WESTWARD the BELLS

CHRISTIAN CIVILIZATION MOVES WESTWARD
WITH
FATHER JUNIPERO SERRA

alba house
A DIVISION OF THE SOCIETY OF ST. PAUL
STATEN ISLAND, NEW YORK 10314

WESTWARD
the BELLS

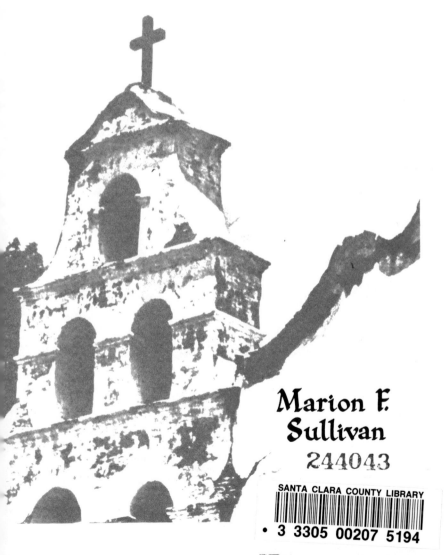

Marion F. Sullivan

Nihil Obstat
    Daniel V. Flynn, J.C.D.
    Censor Librorum

Imprimatur
    Joseph P. O'Brien, S.T.D.
    Vicar General, Archdiocese of New York
    May 18, 1971

The nihil obstat and imprimatur are official declarations that a book or pamphlet is free of doctrinal or moral error. No implication is contained therein that those who have granted the nihil obstat and imprimatur agree with the contents, opinions or statements expressed.

ISBN: 0-8189-0218-3

Library of Congress Catalog Card Number 75-169139

Designed, printed and bound in the U.S.A. by the Pauline Fathers and Brothers of the Society of St. Paul, 2187 Victory Blvd., Staten Island, N.Y. 10314 as part of their communications apostolate.

DEDICATED
to my husband
C. EDWARD SULLIVAN

PREFACE

*T*HE STORY of Father Junipero Serra has been many times told. But perhaps today, as never before, his impressive works and magnanimous soul radiate drama on the stage of history and stir the hearts of men. For as we look into the past, we see in the life of this illustrious leader a poignant relationship to our own problems, the problems of today, tomorrow and always.

I wish to express particular gratitude to the Academy of American Franciscan History and especially to Father Maynard Geiger, O.F.M., Ph.D., and to Father Antonine Tibesar, O.F.M., Ph.D., whose tireless research and fine works have not only revealed new facts but clarified old ones. To the many others close to me, who have given their help, advice and encouragement, I am most grateful and I wish to give special mention to my friend and faithful helper, Mrs. Evelyn Ullrich.

I have attempted to emphasize Serra's heritage and the motivating forces that destined him to push Christian civilization to the far Pacific shores of the North American continent. And the ancient bells of Palma echo their song of love today in San Diego, Santa Barbara and Carmel.

CONTENTS

ILLUSTRATIONS

David Muench

Bells echoed their song through history, moving westward with Christian civilization. This tower might have been found in Palma. Actually, it is part of the old Mission San Carlos de Borromeo at Carmel, California.

INTRODUCTION

*T*HE APPEARANCE of a new and fresh appreciation of the life of Father Junipero Serra is most appropriate at this time when we have celebrated the bicentennial of the coming of Christianity to California and when the Bishops of the United States have with unanimous vote petitioned the Holy Father, Pope Paul VI, to expedite the examination of the evidence of the heroic virtues of this humble Friar and to judge if he should not be venerated as one of God's chosen and blessed servants.

The story of the life and labors of the Apostle of California has been told many times, and well. The historians who have been attracted to write of his life and times have recounted the story with various emphases. Some have been most interested in the political problems of the Spanish occupation and the relations of missionary Friars with the changing attitudes of the civil government toward them and toward their Indian charges. Others have dwelt upon the resources of the Golden State, its fascinating geography and topography, and the carefree life of its original inhabitants. Many have been captivated by the art and architecture of the twenty-one missions, so lovingly preserved by Californians and so attractive to tourists.

Since the classic biography of Serra by his confrere, Father Palou, none, I believe, has so well understood Junipero Serra as a person, as the author of this volume. Marion F. Sullivan has given us not only an excellent historical record but also a rare insight into Serra's mind and heart. No other appreciation of the little Majorcan's life reveals so well to the modern mind the deep wellsprings of his dynamic zeal — in a word, his personal sanctity. This is clearly a labor of love.

When, as we hope, the Holy See gives official recognition to that extraordinary goodness which was apparent to the Indians who called him "The Holy Father," this book will provide the understanding and appreciation which our personalistic age demands for its heroes.

Joseph T. McGucken
Archbishop of San Francisco
January 19, 1971

Church of Santiago at Jalpan, the only remaining structure built by Father Serra. Intricate detail and design indicate unusual architectural and artistic skill.

WESTWARD the BELLS

CHAPTER I
LETTERS OF GOLD

a BELL RANG OUT at dawn — calling Angelus. Then from the distant hills, from the great cathedral, from more than half-a-hundred churches, convents and chapels in and around the Mediterranean city of Palma they resounded. Round, solemn, resonant bells, sharp, blithe, soprano bells mingling with tiny tinkling chimes, vibrated, bounded and rolled over red-tiled flat-roofed houses, colorful gardens, Islamic domes and Gothic towers, drifting down to the curving shores of the sparkling aqua bay, to fade beyond — somewhere in the western sea.

Chroniclers of the day, they would ring intermittently for morning masses, a wedding, a funeral or to proclaim news of importance. Life in Palma synchronized with bells. Today they seemed to ring with intensity as though anticipating drama for the capital city of Majorca.

1

Father Junipero Serra had long since risen from his narrow plank bed. As long as he could remember, his days had been regulated by the reassuring immutability of bells. The dim light of early morning crept in to reveal the barrenness of his monastery cell in the Convent of St. Francis, as he knelt in prayer. Like an undulant sea, his mind was surging with tumultuous cross currents. But the vital problems dominating his consciousness were personal. Consequently, he left them to the ultimate plan of God and turned his immediate attention to the neatly formulated program of the day.

It was January 25th, the Feast Day of Blessed Ramon Lull. In 1749, as they had for four hundred years, all Spain would turn back her romantically historic pages to honor the loved national hero and Christian martyr. But Majorcans regarded this as one of the greatest celebrations of the year. Lull was their own native son. Born in Palma in 1235, he was buried in the church of St. Francis, next door to the Convent. The annual festivities provided a tangible testament of their personal affection for this man who was so real to them.

Usually tranquil Palma bustled with activity. Most everyone was hanging banners, arranging flower festoons, polishing or furbishing the already neat, gem-like little city. It must sparkle! Guests of importance would be coming. The celebration would be no boisterous, noisy fiesta. Music and dancing would come later, but the morning activities, in keeping with their intention, would be religious, patriotic and academic.

Though most Palmans had no direct contact with the University, it represented their aspirations. They loved the venerable institution and its traditions. It had given Palma much of its character and its charm. Named for its founder, the fifteenth century Lullian University of Palma was officially recognized in 1673 by Pope Clement X, with the impressive title "Pontifical Imperial Royal and Literary University of Majorca." For the sake of simplicity, however, it was generally known as the University of Palma.

Whatever her title, the University on this day, as it had each year, would flash her elegance and splendor in traditionally dramatic pageantry. Reliving valiant and heroic deeds performed for God and country, she would coordinate the cherished past with the vital present, making them one in the living spirit of the Holy Catholic Faith, the life, the soul of the Spanish world.

Other cultural centers of the world would listen for reports of the theological dissertation. Rome, Oxford, Madrid, Paris and the people of Majorca were asking, "Who is to be the speaker of the day?" Always, it was one of the vital speeches of the year. This year, chosen for the honor was the illustrious head of the Department of Theology at the Lullian University of Palma, Friar Minor of the Order of St. Francis, the Reverend Doctor Junipero Serra.

News traveled fast, even in 1749. Nobles, statesmen, intellectuals, guildsmen, farmers, laborers, everyone applauded the choice. They knew this brilliant educator, this leading and widely acclaimed intellectual theologian, this warmly loved, humble son of St. Francis. A native of Petra, twenty-five miles away, Serra had come to Palma with his parents in his early teens. Now, thirty-five, he had spent more than half his life in the lovely center of Christian devotion, culture and knowledge. Under the gentle guidance of learned Franciscans, he had graduated from novice to priest, from student to distinguished professor, eminent scholar and eloquent speaker.

Majorcans knew Serra and he knew them. They loved the jovial Franciscan. His easy manner, his kindness and his quick natural sense of humor made him one of them. Only about five feet two inches tall and pleasantly plump, his kindly rotund face framed large brown, twinkling eyes that could reach into the depths of another's with thoughtful concern and loving understanding.

Father Serra never sought personal honors, glory or fame. He seemed to be unaware of the aura of acclaim attributed to him. Furthermore, even those who ardently sang his praises could not even comprehend his profound capacity for love. For from love alone emanated his words of wisdom.

For generations Serra's people had lived by the soil and his academic life had never lessened the oneness of spirit originating from this valuable heritage. The hope of budding spring, the cruel deprivation of drought, the rewarding satisfaction of an abundant harvest, the suffering, the tragedy of plague, all were bred in the roots and blood of agrarian Majorcans. This heritage, this intimate contact with nature, one of his greatest riches, not only united Serra with the people of his home land, but would in the years to come become an invaluable source of physical and moral strength.

Outshining all other qualities, was his glowing religious zeal, which engendered warmth and understanding, compassion and tenderness reaching from the pulpit to the cries and heartaches of his people. In the classroom and throughout the entire island, when lenten missions or special feast

Crucifix of the Spanish era.

day sermons had taken him to the other cities and villages of Majorca, his words reached into the souls of men, bringing them peace and communion with God. Crowds filled the churches when he spoke. They strained to hear every word, then told their friends about the Franciscan with the resonant, musical voice, yet so strangely gentle, who could "talk on anything from rocks to eternity." [1]

This appointment as speaker for the festivities of Ramon Lull, no doubt, gave Father Serra some natural pleasure, some exaltation of recognition. We can only be certain, however, that he would have accepted it with characteristic humility. The sermon was his responsibility of the day, but Serra's mind, as it had been for months, was in conflict with other problems.

These problems concerned his deepest being, all he had been, all he hoped to be. They challenged his vocation to the priesthood and its essence, the salvation of souls. Vocation is part calling and part listening. He was praying and listening. He was praying and listening and watching for answers.

Even before his novitiate, Serra had read all available script regarding St. Francis and his early companions. Through this medium, these men had become his close friends. This vicarious friendship not only developed a deep reverence for the founders of the Franciscan Order but directed an intense personal desire to bring the Faith to the thousands who had not yet heard the Word of God. He wanted to become a missionary and should God find him worthy, to become a martyr for Christ.

Martyrdom, perhaps, was a daring aspiration. But mis-

1. Geiger, **Life and Times of Junipero Serra**, Vol. VI, p. 33.

sionary work had been the propelling motive of his vocation. It had triggered his application for training, education, every aspect of his intellectual and spiritual development. Paths had opened before him and he followed sedulously, knowing interiorly that all comes from God. The positions he now held, the honors, the esteem were not of his seeking, but natural products of his thirty-five years of activity; fruits following bloom. We can look back and assume they were inevitable.

Serra was no idealistic dreamer. Before he spoke to anyone of his desire, he must be certain it was no personal whim, no urge born of sudden over-zealous fascination. He met the problem in the only way he knew. He prayed. The flames grew. He prayed too, for a companion, someone like himself, who desired missionary work. And each day the calling grew in intensity.

He could foresee his colleagues' reactions, should the news circulate. They would say he was indispensable to the University; no one could replace him; after all these years of Franciscan training, he was obligated to the University; he would be casting away rewards due his life's labors. Greater honors for him were already rumored. And they would say he was too old. This he could not deny. Thirty-five was late to start a new and hazardous career. (The normal life span of that time would leave him only five to ten more years.)

There was another stumbling block. Majorcan priests had been prohibited from missionary work in the New World. It was a political situation. Traditionally independent Majorca had resisted the Spanish Crown, only submitting about 1709. Long ago a Majorcan missionary had failed, giving fuel to nationalistic tempers. Despite the fact that the founder of the missionary movement had been Majorcan, in all these forty years, not one missionary preparatory school had been established in Majorca and no Majorcans had served in the New World. Serra knew the fine army of dedicated and qualified Franciscans who, given the opportunity, would serve valiantly in the field. He knew also, that just because the situation had existed for forty years, did not mean it was impervious to change.

He surveyed the field realistically and made plans. Apprehensions now were giving way to assurance that missionary work was the path for him to follow. Now it was time to act.

First he told his superior. He would need time to find a replacement. Besides, he had political influence, should he be inclined to use it in Serra's favor. No records indicate the superior's reactions to the interview. His later actions, however, suggest that Serra's apprehensions were justified. Serra told no one else. His thoughts were too deeply serious for idle discussion, alarm or fanfare. He pledged his superior to secrecy and awaited developments.

Alone in his cell, Serra weighed these problems, then turned to the task of the day, his talk on Ramon Lull. The saintly fellow Majorcan was one of his favorite heroes. He could hardly have studied history, philosophy and theology without an intimate knowledge of Ramon Lull. To tell others of him would be a natural revelation of inspiring deeds, ideas, and ideals.

Bells shattered the monastic silence. Reverberating through corridors and cloisters, they proclaimed the time, ten o'clock; the hour for the ceremonies to begin.

Members of the faculty, priests, students were milling about the courtyard in aimless confusion. A bugle blast, a sharp command from the Beadle and military order prevailed. Double symmetrical lines of academic caps and gowns formed a sea of dignified black, splashed with silk-lined hoods and drapes of red, blue, purple, gold and white, designating special honors, degrees and departments. Gray robed Franciscans, priests in black cassocks with white albs, first year students in black tailored suits followed, all slowly moving out through the courtyard into the narrow, twisting, tree-lined streets of Palma.

Drums and trumpets flourished into martial music. The Beadle, voice of order and protocol, in rich velvet robe and carrying the mace of authority, led the procession. Behind him the university Rector strode with dignified elegance in long, purple robe, splendidly embroidered in red and gold and trailing a long velvet train carried by a little page staggering under its heavy weight.

Crowds watched as they wound slowly and magnificently through the town and up the hill to the Bishop's palace. Near by the great cathedral, like a majestic fortress, dominated the busy Bay of Palma. Soft sunlight gleamed on the masts of brightly colored fishing boats rolling at anchor below. A salty whiff of sea drifted inland.

In a few moments, his Excellency appeared, radiant in scarlet silken robe with ermine cape, wearing the tall white and gold tiara, crowning symbol of his office and carrying the golden staff of the Shepherd in bold, confident strides. Leading the procession, his Excellency was followed by attendants, the Mayor, aldermen, visiting nobles, government officials and other prominent dignitaries.

Trumpets, drums, stringed instruments accompanied singing minstrels in rousing rhythmic hymns and marching songs. The people of Palma and their guests watched, filling the town square, the narrow streets, overhead balconies, fences, some even perched precariously in trees.

Absorbed by the spectacle, one that had been reenacted perennially for hundreds of years, they were one in spirit. Some may have been drawn by the personal magnetism of an individual. Leaders always arouse casual interest and some were friends. But Majorcans had only perfunctory interest in officials. What set their minds afire was the color, the emblems, symbols of their faith, their history, their heritage, their hopes. History had dealt harshly with these people. Hundreds of years of Moorish persecution, oppression, violent desecration of all that was Christian were still, after centuries of rebirth, vivid memories, keen, living, personal. Not personal hatred, revenge, but pride of Christian victory, determination to keep what was all but lost. Today's procession was an outward expression of gratitude, dedication, renewed enthusiasm for the faith that was their life. To eighteenth century Majorcans, loyalty to the emblem of the Cross superceded loyalty to a flag.

James I of Aragon in 1229 freed Majorca from Moorish occupation and dispersed the hordes of savage, ruthless pirates and buccaneers whose stronghold of plunder and outrage was the Bay of Palma.

Christianity, crushed and forced underground began picking up the pieces. Rebuilding and rejuvenation was a slow, difficult work but with liberation emerged not only the vivification and deepening of Christian faith but a poignant awareness of freedom.

It was this same devotion to the Faith, born of persecution, that had fired the overwhelming zeal for conversion of the entire world to Christianity and had led Spain into her Golden Age. Yet, insular and independent Majorca was only remotely involved in Spain's rise to glory or with the military and political implications that had contributed to her decline.

Majorcans had maintained a profound simplicity of belief, a dogma involving sacraments, sacramentals, redemption, self-sacrifice, penance, prayer and obedience to the laws of God. Fulfillment, as in every society, was subject to the variables of man's nature, the gap between transgression and perfection. But rebellion was unthinkable.

Ramon Lull appealed to the Majorcan spirit. Born of a wealthy courtier just six years after Majorcan liberation, the fiery nobleman had led a life of reckless adventure until his "conversion." Self-alienated from worldly pursuits, he had become equally daring and audacious as a defender of the faith, brilliant scholar, educator, poet, philosopher, recluse and missionary.

At a time when intense hatreds were flaring into violence and atrocities and indelible bitterness gnawed at souls on both sides, he stood like a flaming sword between the Cross and the Crescent. His was a sword of peace and love. Lull went into the heart of Islam Africa, lived with the enemy, learned his language, studied his books and succeeded in converting Arabs to Christianity. He hoped by physical contact, intellectual understanding and selfless love to close the gap of hundreds of years of anguish. He hoped, too, to tap the vast store of knowledge of mathematics, engineering, astronomy, chemistry, medicine and other sciences accumulated through Arab conquests of successive civilizations. This knowledge he hoped to bring home to Spanish schools and universities. In return, Islam's reward would be the Christian faith. "Not to love is death and love is life,"[2] was the motto for which he lived and died. But above all, he longed to end the long-standing enmity between Arab and Spaniard. But Islam would not buy his plan. He did make hundreds of converts. He transported much of the knowledge which was inculcated in Spanish schools. But at the age of eighty-one, he was killed by Arabs and in 1316 he was buried in the lovely church of St. Eulalia, known in Serra's time, as St. Francis of Palma. Upon these facts Serra would base his sermon.

The procession's arrival at the church was announced by a flutter of drums and trumpeting finale. Each dignitary according to rank, tradition and protocol, was escorted to his place.

Magnificently baroque, the interior of the old church needed no adornment. Conscientious parishioners, however, had adorned the main altar and twenty-one side altars with gaily colored fresh flowers. The walls were draped with silk brocade and banners hung from the ceiling. Thousands of flickering candles illuminated the vast nave, casting wierd shadows in darkened corners. Their light penetrated rolling clouds of incense and disseminated misty, eerie, waves, moving across high rose-colored, stained glass windows.

Solemn High Mass began. The mesmeric pace of the ritual of that ancient traditional ceremony, which daily re-enacts the drama of salvation, was accentuated by the chanting of Majorca's finest choir. The officiating priest sang the Gospel in rhythmic climactic tones, then it was time for the sermon.

2. Daniel Rops, **Cathedral and Crusade**, p. 512.

Father Serra climbed the semicircular stairway, leading to a small cupular pulpit on the right wall above and just beyond the sanctuary. All was quiet. In anticipation, everyone looked toward the speaker. He was very small up there alone, his shoulders hardly clearing the missal stand. But the depth, strength, and volume of his musical voice drew full attention. No one regarded stature as all surrendered to the sonorous voice that rose and fell in rhythmic eloquence.

The sermon, Father Palou said, was "dramatic and eloquent." We know it was one of Serra's finest. It won applause far and wide. Thirty years later, Father Palou, Serra's dear friend and biographer, wrote that he had heard one of the professors remark, "This sermon is worthy of being printed in letters of gold."

We can not record the words. Unfortunately, they are lost to posterity. But sermons fit only a given time and circumstance. We can be certain, however, that they rang with his apostolic zeal, his dynamic personality, his profound simplicity.

This was the pinnacle of Serra's academic career. Open to him were greater honors, a bishopric, perhaps, assignment as Rector of the University, Provincial Superior of the Order of St. Francis.

But Father Serra was not born to accumulate honors, praise, high positions. He was foreordained for other goals. As the sun set on the ceremonies, this day would mark the climax of his achievements in the eastern hemisphere and destine the beginning of adventures he could neither plan nor conceive.

CHAPTER II
HOME IS A SEMINARY

*T*HE QUIET, SERENE, farming village of Petra was snuggling in a fertile valley between Majorcan hills about twenty-five miles inland from Palma. Most everyone was asleep that November night in 1713. Only in the square stone house at No 6 Barracar Avenue a light was burning.

Margarita Serra was in labor. This was not her first child. Since their marriage, Margarita Ferrer and Antonio Serra had had two children, a boy and a girl. Both had died in infancy. For nine long months Margarita had hoped and prayed that this time all would be well. Still apprehension grew as the pains accelerated through the long, cruel, anxious hours.

Then at one o'clock in the morning, there was a cry, the unmistakable cry of an infant. The Serras had a boy! He seemed to be a normal baby, small, a bit on the frail side, but apparently healthy. Previous experience, however, had left sharp wounds.

The devout parents were keenly aware that this new fragile bit of life, too, could be snatched from them. Helpless before the dim intangible of Miguel's earthly survival, they took prudent precautions to assure his eternal joy as a baptized son of Christ. As soon as morning came, Antonio saw the padre and arranged for baptism that very day, the 24th of November. The name was no problem. They would call him Miguel, as they had their first son.

The simple baptism complied with the essential formal religious traditions and protocol but it was brief, small and devout. Only relatives and a few close friends attended. The midwife led the modest procession to St. Peter's church, with Miguel snuggled in her arms. The tiny babe was almost lost in the family heir-loom dress, long, white, elaborately embroidered and trimmed with lace. Around all this finery was wrapped a clean wool blanket to keep him warm. The God-parents walked behind, followed by the others. The Godmother, Sebastian Serra, Antonio's sister, held the baby during the ceremony but returned him to the care of the mid-wife when they left the church. When it was over, Antonio gave the priest some fruit for his trouble, then they all returned to the Serra home. Now, perhaps for the first time, Margarita could see and hold her son. The mid-wife put the baptized Miguel in his mother's arms with the words, "Ja'l vos tornam Cristai," "I return him to you a Christian."[1] The little group sat around the living room, chatted a while, ate some cookies, drank a little wine or brandy. Then each

1. Geiger, **op. cit.**, p. 6.

guest offered a toast to the proud parents. "Congratulations! May God give you joy in him and may he be a good boy."[2]

By now most everyone in the closely knit little town of Petra knew the Serras had a baby boy. What they could not know was that Miguel Serra was destined to be the Apostle of the Holy Catholic Faith — that living, motivating force of Majorcan life, history and tradition — on far western shores, in a land then practically unknown, a land called California.

Alined with the other houses on Barracar Avenue, the Serra home stood flush with the narrow, cobbled street. Centuries old, the plain but sturdy, two-story house, built of stone was probably a wedding gift from the Ferrar family to their daughter. A little roomier than some in the neighborhood, but in most respects it was typical of the farm houses of the area. In front a wide, arched doorway was entrance for the mule, the cart and the family. A square door to the left led to a corridor separating the cart shelter and the mule corral from the rest of the house. The living quarters with cement floor and whitewashed walls were clean, neat and immaculately scrubbed. The parlor was simply furnished with just a table, a couple of chairs, a bench and a chest for linens. The bedroom was just large enough for the bed and a small table. Opening from the living room, an alcove served as kitchen. Consisting mostly of a wide, deep fireplace, it answered the purpose of cook stove, light, heat and the center for family and friendly gatherings. In fact, except for the one small window above the door, the fireplace was the only source of light for that part of the house. Upstairs was another bedroom and a storage room.

2. **Ibid.**

Like most Majorcan families, the Serras farmed their own land. Some writers refer to them as peasants but feudalism was abolished in Catalonia and the Balaerics in the fifteenth and sixteenth centuries. Ownership, established through a long line of ancestors generated love of the land, loyalty, permanence and security.

Approximately in the center of Majorca, Petra was on a fertile plateau. The soil was good, some of the best on the agricultural island. Life was gratifying, but it was rough. The people worked hard. A man's returns depended on his own initiative, his muscular ability to coax from the earth its maximum production and nature's response to his urging, to the rain and the sun and the renewal of spring. Still, they held no illusions, no soaring hopes, for well they knew spring could be a bounteous benefactor or a cruel tyrant. All had seen abundant crops smashed before the wrath of an unseasonal storm or seared from merciless drought. Majorcans were conditioned to hardship. They were stolid, patient, forbearing, and full of fun and grace.

Majorcans were not essentially Spanish. Extremely insular, they were a mixture of races and characteristics. Drawn together by similar problems and interests, free from status complexities and the sham of sophistication, they faced realities in mutual awareness. Life was simple. Their food, mostly produced on the farms was plain but usually plentiful. Generally speaking, they were robust, vigorous people of good stature. They strode with a calm, natural grace and the dignity of a proud heritage, enhanced by the charm of a ready, friendly smile. And beneath the hardy physical exterior fused a virile vivacity. Life was not dull. Entertainment usually centered around the home or community. Naturally gay spirits could spontaneously burst into exhilaration of

A trailless, rugged terrain.

clear, musical song or exciting, fast-paced graceful dancing.

Education was limited but they were eager to learn. Tales of heroism and courage became tradition as they passed from generation to generation in family and friendly gatherings around the hearth fire. Historically, militarily and culturally Majorcans were closely tied to Catalonia. "Mallorquin," the native language, is related to Catalan and Majorcan and Catalan soldiers for hundreds of years fought side by side against the common enemy.

Iberians, the original inhabitants of the islands, joined by the Celts forming the Celtiberian civilization, thrived for hundreds of years. As early as 1200 and 1000 B.C. they traded with the Phoenicians and learned from them, among other things, the art of sea-faring. From successive Carthaginian and Roman occupation, Majorcans absorbed new arts, crafts and learning. In the age of their Mediterranean ascendancy, the Greeks built trading posts in Majorcan ports. Greek arts, crafts and skills penetrated Majorcan culture but there was no known Greek occupation. Their conquerors and visitors left certain inherited physical characteristics, but amazingly, the inhabitants of the island remained predominantly Majorcan.

Majorcan fighters were renowned for their skill as sling shot operators and in the course of the Carthaginian wars, both Hannibal and Scipio vied for their assistance. Virgil and Livy romanticized on Majorcan sharpshooting power and Julius Caesar used them in his conquest of Gaul.

Despite the depradation of invading vandal hordes in 455, civilization continued to advance until the 700's. Then Arabs in a sudden, brazen and prodigiously successful assault conquered the "Isle of Calm," as they called their prize. This was eighty years after the Moorish offensive of

Spain and Northern France. Although Majorca's occupation came late and her liberation was more than two-hundred years before Spain's final victory at Granada, those devastating centuries of Moorish tyranny, persecution and murder were still vividly alive in Christian Majorcan minds.

Islam's pandemic scourge of western civilization was tragedy for the followers of the Cross. Europe stood by helpless before the burning, plunder, rape and devastation. Her wealth, her church, her classical tradition, the civilization of a thousand years were wiped out by the Moslem deluge. Counter-attack was disorganized, slow and uncertain. And Palma Bay, the lovely sheltered Mediterranean cove, was base and lair for the brutal, blood-thirsty Barbary pirates of the sea.

Resistance took on the luster of a crusade and each century marked some gradual retreat of the Moors. "... The men who recovered Spain, Sicily and the Balaerics, who stood at arms, century after century... between the Mass and Koran.... They were the men who not only permitted Europe to survive but who gave it its permanent character," declares Hilaire Belloc in *Towns of Destiny*. Finally on New Year's Eve, 1229, twenty year old King James I of Aragon, with a great fleet, attacked Palma. Leading a force of twenty thousand Majorcans, Catalans and French, four-thousand of whom were knights of the Crusades, he stormed the enemy strongholds, routed the pirates and subjugated the flashing swords of Islam.

This prolonged, violent struggle for freedom unified the independent provinces of the Spanish peninsula. Diverse in interests and language, they were forged into a driving sense of universalism with one common enemy, one faith, one kingdom. Final victory in 1492 released a stupendous impulse of Christian unity and Catholic Spain emerged as the first great European nation to attain full stature. It launched Columbus, with Isabella's blessing, and illumined her Golden Age. A consistent alloy of Christian determination to unite for victory and freedom motivated her audacious progression of discovery, expansion and conquest. It inspired her prodigious effort to civilize, educate and christianize the New World.

The ideal of fusing the power of the state into a militant drive for the preservation and extension of the Faith, originally essential and noble in purpose, did, however, in later years, result in the dangerous and impractical union of Church and State, which would ultimately destroy and restrict much that it had accomplished.

The amazing and swift success of Spain's enterprise has filled the pages of history. But Spain's sun was setting when Miguel Serra appeared on the scene. In 1700 Phillip V of Angou, a Bourbon, grandson of Louis XIV, ascended the throne. With a French king in Madrid and French revolutionary ideas filtering into Spain's fortress of Christianity, the missionary movement was feeling the shackling restraint of imperialism.

The Treaty of Utrecht, signed in 1713, sealed Phillip's victory over the House of Hapsburgh in the war of succession and gave Portugal, Gibralter and Minorca to England. Catalonia and Majorca, both still independent kingdoms, refused to recognize Phillip as their sovereign. Later, in August of 1713, three months before Miguel was born, six Spanish vessels sailed into Palma Bay demanding Majorcan submission. Majorcans fought and won but two years later they signed the articles of capitulation. Majorca suffered for her stubborn resistance and it was this political malediction that subscribed substantially to the rejection of Majorcan Franciscans for missionary work.

By 1749 Spain's hour of glory was weakening. Still a vigorous reconstruction program flourished at home and abroad. An amazing advance in cultural enterprise throughout the entire Spanish domain was manifest in an accelerated building of new churches, monasteries, schools and great universities. The eighteenth century dawned on a world stimulated and excited by a progression of education, art, science and letters.

And before Spain's westward movement should die, one great figure would rise to animate anew that religious fervor which had spurred the original missionary spirit and would light the embers of civilization and faith on far Pacific shores.

As Miguel toddled around his home in Petra, he was happily oblivious of the fundamental and mysterious antecedents that had set the stage of his world and would play so great a part in molding his natural and spiritual graces.

Miguel was three when a sister, Juana Maria, born January 1716, joined the family group. The two little ones played and grew up together but of Margarita and Antonio's five children, only these two survived. Another little girl, Martina Maria, was born four years later, but died very young.

We can look back and see that Miguel's character was being formed in the earliest years of his childhood. The priests at St. Bernardine's and St. Peter's were close family friends. They frequently visited at the Serra home and Miguel saw them at Mass. At Margarita's knees he learned his prayers and through her example, training, influence and love he acquired a deep and lasting love for the Blessed Mother. Both parents implicitly believed and taught their children that life was a gift of God and that it was the primary purpose of each individual to serve Him. Theirs was the comforting security of total belief: no dissent, no questioning, no theorizing, no fulminating. They accepted their Catholicism as divine truth, complete, dependable, holy; won through sacrifice, blood and the Cross. It was theirs to hold, to defend, to share.

Although neither Margarita nor Antonio could read or write, both held a high regard for education and were determined that their son should have every opportunity to learn. At an early age Miguel showed evident signs of being an exceptionally bright boy. Education at that time was available to almost any boy, with or without money if he had the will and the inclination to learn. Antonio needed a son to help on the farm. But his desire that Miguel should have the best educational and religious training superceded all selfish interests.

St. Bernardine's, called the pearl of all the churches of the province (excepting St. Francis of Palma), built in 1607, was only a block from Miguel's home. Smaller than St. Peter's, but with more slender delicate lines, it was truly a gem for a town of fifteen hundred to two thousand people. Though rich in detail and design, the interior was pleasingly delicate. The central, main high altar and each of the ten side altars were gilded. Fine carvings, statues and paintings, all works of intricate Romanesque art, perfected the lovely design.

Next to the church, the Franciscans had built a Friary and school for boys. (No one seemed concerned with education for girls at that time.) To live practically next door to so fine a school was most fortunate for Miguel. He quickly absorbed mathematics, Latin, reading, writing and religion in the friendly and benevolent environment. From the first, the monks recognized in this boy a natural talent for music. They asked if he would like to join them in the choir and almost before he could read, his pure, clear musical tones joined the monks in Divine Office and Gregorian Chant.

After school and on vacations Miguel could help at home with the planting, cultivating, harvesting and caring for the animals. Under Antonio's direction and companionship, he witnessed nature's mysterious promise and fulfillment. He could observe that within a hard shell, a tiny seed pushed tender shoots through firm soil and new leaves opened to the warmth of the sun. Synchronically hidden hairlike roots plunged and spread through the earth seeking nourishment and a plant grows to maturity, multiplying and producing its own kind a hundredfold. This magical responsive co-operation of nature, man and the Creator would become a vital part of Miguel's inner being.

Among other things, he learned that fundamental to any type of farming operation were good rich, deep soil, an abundant water supply and favorable climatic conditions. This early orientation to the land and its practical application would in later years prove indispensable to the success of his goals.

But Miguel's interests began to turn away from the soil. At fifteen, he decided to become a Franciscan. Too young for admission as a novice (the minimum age was sixteen), he decided to enter the preparatory study course. This meant leaving home. The nearest training school and Franciscan seminary was in Palma.

Consequently, one September day in 1729, Miguel, Margarita and Antonio left the family home in Petra, each poignantly aware that this was the first tearing apart of those close, happy years together. The acutely agonizing pain and suffering of separation was to the Serras, as in most sincerely religious families, sorrow mixed with joy. Over and above their own personal emotions was the profound gratitude that their son had been chosen for so noble a calling in the service of God.

Historians only say that they "rode" to Palma. No one tells us by what means they "rode" but it would be natural to assume that they hitched the family mule to their cart parked in the shed next to the parlor and jogged along the hot, dry, dusty twenty-five miles of rough, narrow, winding roads.

As they approached the walled city, they could see the massive towers of Palma's gothic cathedral looming majestically against the sky. The charming city of about thirty-thousand people, sloped semi-circularly from the mountains to the sparkling blue bay. Besides the cathedral, Palma boasted of architecturally perfect "La Longa," center of trade, La Almudiana, the Moorish castle, the Bishop's palace, the College of Sapeinta, the Lullian University and sixty churches and chapels. One of the most beautiful of these was the church and monastery of St. Francis, founded in 1232. This was where Miguel was to register. Their journey was completed. Miguel said goodbye to his parents and Margarita and Antonio then turned and made their way slowly back to Petra.

Three months after his sixteenth birthday, Miguel made formal petition for admission to the Order. This meant a personal interview with the Provincial. At last the day came. Miguel stood before the Very Reverend Fray Antonio Perello Marques and saw a dominant, influential and distinguished leader; a gentle, brilliant, kindly and spiritual man. The Provincial looked down on a very small boy. He was surely too small to be sixteen and certainly too weak and sickly for the strenuous training of the novitiate. Thinking of the boy's welfare, his own responsibilities for the entire group, and no doubt, suspicious of a lie concerning Miguel's age, the Provincial refused admission.

This was a bitter blow to Miguel. Yet his disappointment was dulled somewhat by the inspiration of meeting this fine man. His determination was firmer than before to pursue his vocation. He asked friends to intercede for him. In time, they convinced the Provincial that Miguel was indeed sixteen and that his eagerness and enthusiasm would compensate for his lack of physical strength.

On September 14, 1730 Miguel was invested with the long gray habit and hood of the Franciscan Order at the Convento Santa Maria de los Angeles de Jesus. This small unassuming monastery, with the long name, was ideally located for a novitiate, in a peaceful, secluded spot in the silence of the woods outside the city's walls.

He was still too short to reach the lectern and too weak for certain physical exercises. But it was a happy year and perhaps one of the most important in molding the man.

His freedom from certain chores gave him time to read. *The Chronicles of Our Seraphic Order,* the story of the lives of the saintly men who founded the order became a part of him. He knew them as living friends. He told his fellow students of their colorful episodes, their hopes, their character and the love that motivated all their actions: to seek nothing from this world, to trust all to God and to convert the whole world to the teaching of Christ. He longed to be like them. These were not the vain musings of youth. They were fundamental to his becoming the man God had destined him to be.

After one more year of self-sacrifice and rigorous discipline, on September 15th, 1731, Miguel, with his fellow novices knelt before their Provincial and took the vows of poverty, chastity and obedience. Each had the privilege of taking a name other than his own. Miguel chose the name of the jolly extrovert, Junipero "out of devotion to this holy companion of St. Francis, his deeds of holy simplicity and supernatural charm." [3] Often in later years, he told his dear friend Father Palou, "all good things came to me with profession" and he renewed his vows each year. "With my profession I gained health and strength and grew to medium size, for which I give infinite thanks to God." [4]

Now that he was a Franciscan, Fray Junipero Serra would have to study six more years before he could be ordained a priest. He was moved back to Convento de San Francisco, where he had registered two years before. Here he delved into the intensive study of philosophy and theology. The Latin classics and Scriptures were etched into his memory, ready and alive to be quoted in sermons throughout his life.

He reached for wisdom and learning as ladders to truth and to God. The Book of Wisdom pretty well expresses Serra's serious love of books. "I prayed and prudence was given to me; I pleaded and the spirit of Wisdom came to me ... the riches I do not hide away. For to men she is an unfailing treasure; those who gain this treasure win the friendship of God." [5]

His reputation as earnest student and remarkably fine speaker was spreading outside monastery walls. The title of

3. Palou, **Life of Junipero Serra** — G. W. James, p. 3.
4. **Ibid.**
5. Book of Wisdom, 7:7-14.

Doctor of Philosophy earned for him a position of university professor and parish priests from other Majorcan cities were asking him to preach on special feast days.

In Serra's time the sermon was more than a homily. There was no television, no radio, very little outside entertainment. The sermon was the center of information, sometimes news. The spoken word was all important. People listened reflectively, evaluating, dissecting, appraising. Serra's sermons electrified his audiences with enchanting bits of science, history, anecdotes and Scotus philosophy. He understood his fellow Majorcans and his profound love for them reached into their souls, drawing them closer to friendship with the saints, the Blessed Mother and our Lord.

In the winter of 1737 he was ordained. Father Junipero Serra would be a priest forever. In the eighteen years since the frail little boy, who had come with Margarita and Antonio from the farm in Petra to Palma he had grown physically, spiritually and intellectually. He had made close friends in the monastery, the closest of whom were his former pupils, Fray Francisco Palou and Fray Juan Crespi, now fellow priests of the Order.

He spent twelve more busy, hard working years in Palma teaching, speaking, training young aspirants for the priesthood, and as eminent Lullian University professor, Doctor of Philosophy and Doctor of Theology. But in 1749 the heralded Ramon speaker whose words "should be printed in letters of gold" would spurn honors for the greater love of the Cross.

"Home is the seminary of all other institutions."[6] Margarita and Antonio had done their work well. Their exem-

6. E. H. Chapin.

plary counsel "to serve God alone" and St. Francis' code "glory only in the Cross of Christ" had piloted the boy to manhood and the man to the top of religious and scholastic service in his native Majorca. But the walls of security and established culture were not to hold this bold spirit. From his earliest years the Cross had been the symbol of impassioned love that embraced all humanity, its sufferings, its needs, its wants. Now the spark of fragile life that had glowed one November night on Barracar Avenue thirty six years ago burned in a magnanimous love that transcended native boundaries, culture and fixed customs. It was reaching out to a multitude of souls living in pagan darkness, entangled in hopeless ignorance, filth and despair. Serra, the priest, the professor, the apostle would bring them new ways to live, news ways to think and the hope and light of Truth.

CHAPTER III
NEW WORLDS FOR OLD

a FEW WORDS SPOKEN in confidence, a personal letter intercepted, a bit of private conversation overheard and a rumor starts — even in monastic halls. Father Serra presumed that all he had told of his missionary aspirations was securely locked in the confidence of his superior. But superiors have aides and walls have ears. How, or from what source secretive whisperings grew into rumored news — no one knows.

But one day there was a knock on Father Palou's cell door. His friend, Father Raphael Verger had news. One of their own priests, someone right here at St. Francis' was going to the New World as a missionary. No. He didn't know who.

Dazzled, but managing to suppress his excitement, Father Palou dismissed his friend as quickly as courtesy allowed and went into a reverie. Palou, city bred, had the acumen and fine Spanish features of an intellectual. At first it seemed impossible. If it were true, who was this intrepid priest who dared challenge the powers that be. Perhaps that was all that was needed to shatter the stupid thirty-six year old ban. Palou's concern reached beyond curiosity or politics. Since seminary days he had discouraged the compelling desire within him to become involved in missionary work. How many other Majorcan vocations had been alienated by this political tyranny? Time generates changes. Palou's hopes flared anew. How could he reach the one whose daring exceeded custom? Two applications could have a double impact. Answers did not come to calm his turmoil and he automatically turned to work and prayer.

Days passed. Then, another knock. Father Serra, his closest friend wanted a few words with him. The two had first met as student and professor, but despite Serra's seniority, their friendship ripened into a strong indissoluble union of understanding and mutual affection. Palou promptly disclosed Verger's news and his own secret ambitions. It was a poignant moment for the two men as they looked at each other in profound comprehension.

"The rumor is true. I am the one," Serra said, then added, "Just now I have resolved to come to invite you to go along on this journey; ever since I resolved to go, in my heart I felt an inclination to speak to you, as I was led to believe you were interested."[1] If this was a great moment between the two friends who were united in the presence of Christ and who regarded prayer as real as the sunrise and the morning dew, then it too was a page of history for the

1. Palou, James, p. 7.

Valley south of Eseñada. Miles and mountain ranges to cross before reaching their goal.

New World. As a team, they would work in mutual commitment to the fulfillment of their common, complex goal.

Both agreed that secrecy was essential to the consummation of their project. Already they had verification that a word or sign could spark a proliferation of rumor that might destroy their hopes before they were given a chance to materialize.

Serra set the wheels in motion. All details regarding the foreign missions were handled by a central governmental agency in Madrid. He wrote Fray Matias de Velasco, Commissary General of the Indies, requesting missionary assignment for Palou and himself. He purposely made no territorial specifications. At that time, Franciscans were active in Mexico, Peru, the Philippines and all lands under Spanish domain.

His letter arrived in Madrid at a propitious moment. Two commissaries from Mexico had just arrived for the specific purpose of selecting missionaries for the New World. Fr. Velasco, nevertheless, sent a cold, deliberate letter to Serra, stating that all quotas were filled and that, in fact, sixty-three missionaries were standing by in Cadiz, waiting for ships to take them across the Atlantic.

Serra knew that intervals between Atlantic sailings were from six months to a year and regarded Velasco's letter as a rejection. One slight ray of hope, however, left some encouragement. Velasco added that should vacancies occur, he would think of them.

The promise was vague and Serra, a man of action, wrote the apostolic missionary preparatory college on the mainland, requesting application for admission for two.

Letters traveled slowly and Serra had work to do. Lent began on February nineteenth. It was the custom for parish priests to invite a special guest speaker for the penitential sermons and instructions. Petra invited Serra. As Serra accepted this unexpected opportunity, he was deeply grateful for this generous gift in the divine drama, this last visit to his home town before leaving this part of the world forever. The old Franciscan monastery of San Bernardino, endeared by happy childhood memories, was his home through those delightful last days in Petra.

In the meantime, things were happening in Madrid. Five of the prospective missionaries who had been waiting in Cadiz defected. Political pressure may have penetrated high places. In any case, the commission agreed to accept Serra's and Palou's applications. After deliberate consideration — no doubt pressed by demands for priests from Mexico and by drop-outs from the continent — the Spanish commissary released the out-dated Majorcan ban and sent assignment papers to both priests for missionary work in New Spain. But neither Palou nor Serra received the papers.

The commissar's messenger delivered them to the monastery but for reasons of his own, the superior tucked them away in his desk. This is a little difficult to understand. No doubt, his was an impulsive act, goaded by the barren hope that his two top men might become discouraged and give up the plan. Understandably, too, he must have feared that once the news was out that the ban was lifted, a rash of requests for missionary work would leave serious vacancies in his well organized establishment. After an unreasonable period of frustration in both Palma and Madrid, the commissary, suspecting foul play, tried again. This time he gave explicit orders to place the papers personally in the hands of either Palou or Serra. No one else!

Palm Sunday, on the thirteenth of March, tingled with the sparkling spring beauty of a glorious Mediterranean morning. Palou, deep in meditation, was walking to the chapel for the blessing of the palms when suddenly someone rushed up to him excitedly chattering a confusion of words, whose purport was "a personal messenger is here with important papers for you."[2]

Palou, at long last, with the assignments in his hand, went to the superior. Defeated in his futile intrigue, the superior gave permission and Palou immediately left for Petra.

Later, when he wrote the biography of Serra, Palou (who never refers to himself) says of Serra, it was, "for him a source of greater joy and happiness than if he had received a royal decree naming him to some bishopric."[3]

At St. Bernardine's that night, the lights burned late as the two friends discussed plans. Since no imminent trans-Atlantic sailing was scheduled, there was time for Serra to complete his mission at Petra. Palou would take care of the necessary details. He sent their acceptances to the commissary, arranged for replacements and other affairs pertinent to leaving St. Francis, made reservations for transportation to Cadiz, the official port of departure and rendezvous for missionaries to the New World. Both agreed it was still best not to discuss their plans with those not involved.

It would be a sacrifice not to share his elation with his parents but he sensed that the shock would be too much if they were aware that this farewell embrace would be his last goodbye. Neither of the missionaries wanted emotional

2. **Ibid.**
3. **Ibid.**

demonstrations, bally-hoo, eulogy nor adulation. They wanted only to slip quietly from the scene and get on with the work to be done.

Established customs rarely changed in that part of the world. As they had on every Tuesday morning after Easter for hundreds of years, most everyone in Petra assembled at St. Peter's for the final ceremonies that completed the Lenten and Easter observances. They loved Serra because he was one of Petra's sons and because, as visiting priest on recurring occasions, he had relighted their professed faith with new hope and love.

Serra led the traditional procession as all solemnly sang, prayed and marched up the zig-zag path to the shrine of Mare de Bon Any, atop the hill. Here the faithful came all through the year to pray for the recovery of a loved one, the success of crops, and expectant mothers prayed to St. Anne, the mother of the Blessed Mother of Jesus. Without doubt Margarita had come here thirty-five years before to pray for the physical and spiritual welfare of her child. Now, Margarita, seventy and Antonio, seventy-three, were too feeble to make the trip.

After the ceremonies, as a gesture of appreciation to the visiting priest, each pilgrim knelt and kissed Serra's hand. These were his people, his schoolmates, their wives, their children, his neighbors, his relatives. They could not know that as he looked affectionately into the eyes of each, that their dear friend and priest was saying goodbye to them forever.

From the hilltop shrine, this beautiful April morning, Serra could view a panorama of his native Majorca. Rich, green valleys, neat, church-spired villages nestled among the mountains, mountains that stretched out in every direction, yet always bending to the sea. Directly below was Petra: her square stone houses, set stolidly in rows forming a kind of rectangle with St. Peter's bulky, square tower rising protectively at one end and at the other, St. Bernardine's slender, artistic spire pointing toward heaven. Softening the severity of stone, were spreading shade and fruit trees, gardens flashing color, vineyards sprouting new, brownish-green leaves. Windmills turned lazily in the soft Mediterranean breeze and livestock grazed contentedly in lush meadows. Fenced off in neat declaration of ownership, fields flushed the bright new-green of spring. Beyond was the sea, the unknown, but from this foundation rock of firm, deeply rooted faith would emanate new hope, new vision, new civilizations, people utterly different, with whom he would relate even more intimately than with his own.

When Margarita and Antonio left Miguel at Palma twenty years before, their renunciation had been final. Without benefit of theological reasoning, they had accepted the dull pain, the agony of separation with the true devotion of Catholic parents. But empirical to the vocation was the implied consolation, the comforting certainty that Majorcan priests conventionally remained in Majorca and Majorcan conventions endured. Change was unthinkable. He belonged to Majorca, to them. He would visit them periodically.

After the ceremony Serra did visit them. How he must have cherished those precious moments, crowded with nostalgia: his mother's tender understanding, kindly, simple solicitous precautions; his father's daily practical, sound advice, the unemotional but implacable trust and affection between father and son, and the wisdom imparted in the field and at home.

Not long ago Antonio had become seriously ill and they called Miguel home. Not expecting to recover, Antonio had said to his son, "Miguel, I ask but one thing of you. That is to be a true and faithful Franciscan."[4] Today, no doubt, those words resounded in Serra's mind as the last poignant moments passed. His parents bid, "Adios, Deo to quart de per-ill" ("Goodbye, may God protect you from all danger.").

Then Serra rode the twenty-five miles back to Palma.

Travel wasn't easy in 1749. The first scheduled sailing from Palma direct to Cadiz was months away. In order to save time, they booked passage on a small English freighter, due to sail to Malaga in five days.

By now everyone at St. Francis was alerted that Serra and Palou were leaving. The farewells were tender, sincere and prayerful.

On the Sunday after Easter, the little ship hoisted the English flag, set sail and slipped away, leaving the familiar scenes of Palma and the mountains of Majorca far behind. It had been a busy and emotional week for the two missionaries. They looked forward to a few weeks of rest at sea.

But this was not to be. It seems they were the only passengers aboard. The captain, after his first welcome aboard, turned out to be an argumentative, bullying bigot. He delighted in loud, controversial disputations and jubilantly pounced on the two unsuspecting "Spanish" priests as fair prey. Armed with the minimal primary school compulsory catechetical instruction, he presumed to propound vociferously on all theological subjects. He may have been suffering from a sharp hatred of everything Spanish and Catholic. Feelings between England and Spain were extremely tense

4. Geiger, **op. cit.**, p. 29.

at that time. At any rate, his virulence and violence grew as he persisted in obnoxious argumentation. Palou's admonition that Serra was an eminent and famous Doctor of Theology and Philosophy only fanned his passion and Serra's reluctance to argue added fuel to his infuriated ego. One night Serra awoke to find this mad man at his throat with a knife. Somehow, they survived the two weeks.

Malaga was a welcome port. After three days lay-over, they boarded another ship and after five days of sailing, entered the bustling harbor of Cadiz.

Cadiz, said to be the oldest city in the world and whose name has remained unchanged for over three thousand years, was, in 1749, one of the busiest, most dissolute and cosmopolitan centers of the world. Defended by the sea on one side and inland by massive Roman and Moorish walls, this key port of Mediterranean power had been an age-old focal point of nationalistic bitterness and wars, ancient wars for supremacy of the Mediterranean, then Moorish domination and wars of freedom, wars with England, wars with France. The age of discovery and expansion had made it the gateway to New Spain. Conquistadores, traders, adventurers, soldiers, missionaries departed from the port of Cadiz for New Spain and white sails unfurled to enter the secluded harbor with silver, gold, tobacco, new and strange vegetables and fruits. A thousand ships lay at anchor when Serra's boat slipped unnoticed into the bay. War ships, freighters, fishing boats, ships for the Orient, to bring back spices, silks and ships that plied the Mediterranean ports. Built on a long, narrow strip of land, the "white city" of square, white flat-roofed buildings lay massed against an azure sea.

In the midst of this mundane center of commerce and

crime, power and intrigue, stood the lovely church and monastery of St. Francis, where missionary priests from all the provinces of Spain congregated, waiting for sailing orders. When Fathers Serra and Palou reported to the Father Commissary, Fray Pedro Perez de Mezquia, in charge of assignments, told them that many Spanish priests had defected. Quotas waited to be filled. Father Serra assured the commissary there was no shortage of aspirants in Majorca. The ban was lifted and the rush was on, just as the superior of St. Francis had feared. Many of Serra's friends at St. Francis had confided to Serra their eagerness for missionary work. Credentials were sent to Fathers Juan Crespi, Guillermo Vicens and the news bearer, Father Raphael Verger.

The red tape associated with missionary assignments might be compared to present day government bureaucracy. Though emissaries of the Catholic Church, all missionaries were agents of the State. All missionary work was carried out under government auspices. Transportation and physical support of each missionary was the responsibility of the king. Cumbrous as the arrangement was, it did provide economic and military aid to the missionary movement and without it progress in newly discovered lands would have been impossible. Paradoxically, however, this very entanglement of Church and State eventually led to the collapse of the missions.

Serra and Palou were delayed four months in Cadiz. Serra took this opportunity to write the promised letter to his parents. He addressed it to the parish priest, asking him to read it to them. It was direct, without sentimentality, but beyond the words emanated the consummation of the same mutual faith that had penetrated their lives. He knew they would understand that this was God's will for him and that they would not want him to turn back. He must always go forward, as his vocation directed.

To Father Francesch, to whom it was addressed, he expressed his feelings, "Words cannot express the feelings of affection that overwhelm me, for them who I know are going through a great sorrow. I wish I could give them some of the happiness that is mine, and I feel they would urge me to go ahead and never to turn back. Nothing less than the love of God has led me to leave them."

Delays eventually come to an end. About September first they were off again. Our friends, with eighteen other Franciscans and seven Dominicans boarded the *Villasota* alias *Nuestra Senora de Guadalupe.* (All Spanish ships seemed to bear two names.) It was one of the finest that plied the Atlantic, but when we look at the replicas of those ships we are astounded that forty passengers, plus the crew could endure in the little, top-heavy ship. At the mercy of vascillating winds, it bobbed, rolled and glided south and north, but made a gradual semi-controlled progression westward. Serra said Mass when possible, but was compelled to wait for calm seas, when there was no danger of spilling the sacred wine. Day and night he wore on his breast, the wooden cross, symbol of love and always offered his own inconveniences in devotion to Christ.

The water supply gave out before the middle of October. No chocolate for breakfast, the equivalent of no coffee in our time. They made it to San Juan with no disaster and replenished the supply of water. It meant a delay of several days and Serra, in characteristic zeal, posted announcements for a mission. There was enthusiastic response to the summons of the zealous missionary with the clear, musical voice.

After eighteen days in Puerto Rico, the *Villasota,* well stocked with fruits and supplies left in its wake renewed hope and peace.

Plenty to eat, pleasant seas, all was going smoothly. Then, only one day from their destination, Vera Cruz, a terrifying storm hit with the ferocity of a hurricane. Mast-high waves, torrential rains, savage winds rolled, tossed and dipped the tiny uncontrollable tub mercilessly. Disaster seemed certain. To help matters, the crew mutinied.

Serra remained serenely calm. He called together the missionaries of both orders and proposed a Novena of prayer to St. Barbara. Before the nine days were up, the storm subsided. The valiant little ship was battered and shaken but she had proved her sea-worthiness. She rallied, resumed her course and on December sixth, proudly entered the harbor of Vera Cruz, Mexico.

A Mass of thanksgiving was offered soon after disembarking, then they planned transportation from the eastern seaport to Mexico City, two-hundred and seventy miles inland.

There was little choice. Most followed the customary means of travel: horseback or muleback. Serra chose to walk. Palou had succumbed to the storm and was seriously ill. An Andalusian priest, whose name has been lost in the oblivion of history, accompanied Serra.

Following El Camino Real, the King's Highway, which was no more than a mule trail, they climbed from sea level over mountains seven-thousand-three-hundred-eighty-two feet high, past volcanoes, lakes, across dry plains, tropical jungles and swollen rivers. Mysterious help came to them at crucial times. Several incidents, well known to history, indicate the supernatural. This account, however, is neither a theological discussion nor a proof of sanctity. Suffice to mention that food, shelter and guidance appeared at climacteric moments in regions where no man nor dwelling was thought to exist.

They made the crossing safely and in good health except for one incident. Serra was bitten in the leg by a venomous tropical insect, *Zancudeo,* which they called a mosquito but which literally meant a "small fly." Miriads of poisonous small flies swarmed the tropics. Whatever it was, it left a painful sting, followed by severe swelling and itching. In his sleep, Serra must have scratched it, for it became infected, leaving a permanent ulcerous condition that caused serious suffering the rest of his life.

When Serra arrived at the College of San Fernando in Mexico City, he found Palou recovered and the long, arduous journey from Palma was completed.

Although still known as the New Spain, Mexico had been a thriving province for more than two-hundred years. Great cathedrals, magnificent churches, filled with fine works of art, schools, hospitals, colleges as fine as any in Europe, and the renowned shrine of Our Lady of Guadalupe, testified to the ambitious program and illimitable energy of those who had come to the New World. Pacific seaports flourished. Ships loaded with supplies and treasures from China and the Philippines plied a busy and lucrative trade. But outposts were still inhabited by wild, barbaric savages. Spain, the King and the Church were dedicated to the civilization, not the extermination of these people.

San Fernando College was the training school and general headquarters for preparing priests for the task. Here they equipped themselves with a part of the spiritual and physical stamina required of the vigorous life, the hardships, physical endurance and deprivation of missionary work. They learned the dialects that they might speak to their charges in the tongue natural to them. They learned their habits and customs. Into this framework they would approach them as friends, reach out to them in understanding, coming not as conquerors but as emissaries of the love of Christ.

Serra had left his titles and his honors in Palma. Now, simply Father Junipero, he asked to be admitted to the training courses as a novice. It was his wish to inure himself both physically and spiritually for the task ahead. In his characteristic spirit of asceticism, he offered as penance the austerities and confinement of noviceship. The thirty-six year old Lullian Doctor of Theology submitted freely, enthusiastically, with the fresh zeal of a novice to the confining rules and conformity of a neophyte.

After five months of training, he was given an assignment to missionary work.

CHAPTER IV
THE BUILDER

SIERRA GORDA, northeast of Mexico City, was one of those remote sections of the Spanish New World that after two hundred years of conquest, still presented problems. The nature of the land itself, seemingly argued against progression and easy solutions. Wild, wooded, this mountainous region teemed with tigers, coyotes, deer, countless varieties of venomous snakes, rare, gaily colored tropical birds and myriads of flying and crawling insects. It was rugged, rebellious and full of contrasts: high peaks and deep canyons; intense, humid, oppressive heat and bitter, stinging cold; tempestuous storms that suddenly turned gently flowing streams into raging, flooding torrents and serene, moonlit evenings, singing with cicadas.

Scattered between the folds of the overshadowing mountains were comparatively fertile valleys, where the Pame

Indians scratched the earth, planted and harvested maize corn. Specifically, the Sierra Gorda Pames were known as the Lower Pames, as distinguished from the Upper Pames, in the north around Sonora, but for now, we will simply call them Pames.

Bronze skinned, with thick, flat features and coarse, black hair, the traditionally pagan Pames of Sierra Gorda were considered to be more gentle than their cousins to the north. But hunger or a fuming angry mood, loosening ancient, savage passions, could flare into a screaming, howling raid on a neighboring village and the forest would echo with burning, looting and murdering.

Spasmodic attempts had been made to bring civilizing and Christian influences to the idol worshiping Pames. In the early days of Spanish occupation, Augustinian monks had penetrated the area, brought seeds, taught the rudiments of cultivation and had made some progress toward christianizing the natives. Not until 1740 did they become the responsibility of the Franciscan missionary colleges. Building and expansion in the immense new continent had always demanded more trained men than were available. Still they responded to every call somehow, by spreading thin, turning older provinces over to parish priests and by the constant call for more volunteers from Spain.

Sierra Gorda was a mosquito infested, disease ridden country. Malaria, smallpox, tuberculosis and dysentery had claimed the lives of many of the missionaries who had gone into the isolated area. Consequently, long periods of time elapsed between missionary endeavors and progress had not deeply rooted. The Indian, slow to change habits and customs of thousands of years, easily slipped out of new ways, back to the old. In 1744, ten Franciscans established five

A harsh, solitary land of weird beauty.

missions in Sierra Gorda. Four thousand Indians lived at the missions, worked in the fields and were learning skills and Christian ways, when tragedy struck again. Three of the fathers died in a single month, another soon after. With almost half of their little force gone and the others ill, the project was abandoned.

Again, in 1750, the Guardian of San Fernando called for volunteers for Sierra Gorda. To Serra the call meant that everything was falling into place. Now, less than a year after arriving in the New World, he had completed his San Fernando training. This opportunity for missionary work was what he had been waiting for. At the meeting volunteers were asked for. Eagerly, Serra's voice was heard above the rest, "Here I am. Send me." [1] Secretly, the San Fernando officials had hoped to keep the talented speaker and distinguished theologian in the Mexico City area. Outlying parishes, near and far, constantly demanded intelligent, well educated speakers from San Fernando. But Serra left no doubt in the minds of his superiors that his sole purpose in coming to the New World was missionary service. His good friends, and fellow Majorcans, Fathers Palou and Crespi joined Serra as volunteers for Sierra Gorda. All together, ten made up the group — two for each mission. Serra was appointed president, an honor which, in humility, he declined. Palou served in that capacity for the first year, then Serra assumed those duties.

A remarkable phenomenon of the Spanish American conquest is that slavery was prohibited though there is no doubt that it did exist in certain locations. It is significant in studying the missionary movement to understand that slavery was

1. Geiger, op. cit., p. 100.

contrary to both Spanish law and Catholic doctrine. The motivating ideal of the Spanish dream from the beginning was the Christian principle of human freedom. Queen Isabella had declared, in the days of discovery, that the Indian was a "full and free citizen"[2] and Paul III had issued a Papal Bull to the effect that, "The Indians and all other people, who may later be discovered by Christians are by no means to be deprived of their liberty or the possession of their property."[3]

To enslave and proclaim Catholic doctrine is a direct contradiction. All the teachings of Christ and of the Church are to the effect that "...the Church is the guardian of freedom. The basis of man's freedom is that he is a child of God...redeemed by the blood of Christ and destined for heaven and that no man has the right to interfere with the freedom and dignity of the human person."[4]

Because the Spanish Church and State were bound as one, Spanish practices are often mistaken for Catholic practices and practices of Catholics does not constitute approval by the Church. Salvador de Madariga, the Spanish historian, makes it very clear that under Ferdinand and Isabella the Spanish monarchy, the separate provinces finally united, "became a state and the Spanish state became a church. Not *the* Church. Not the Roman Church."[5] Madriaga speaks from a standpoint of policy rather than doctrine. For the Spanish Church clung intently to Catholic doctrine and due to the reforms and purification of St. Teresa of Avila, St. John of the Cross and the purified form of Fran-

2. Paul Horgan, **Conquistadors**, p. 186.
3. **Ibid**.
4. Richard Walsh, C.S.P., **Religious Freedom in Europe**.
5. Madriaga, **Spain**, p. 25.

ciscans, especially in Majorca, reformation had taken place within the Church in Spain in the sixteenth and seventeenth centuries.

The politics of the Spanish Church, however, were not those of Rome. "The expulsion of the Jews was not a Roman, but a Spanish idea. The Inquisition was controlled by Spain's department of state and outside the jurisdiction of the Church. The royal tendency (of Spain) was to yield as little as possible to papal pressure."[6] But the Church and State combined or separated could only influence, not control human nature. Salvador, Cortez, Pizzarro and other conquistadors contended force was justified to wipe out the horrible customs that they had witnessed among the Aztecs and other tribes of Spanish America: the absolute slavery practiced by rulers of certain native tribes; the horrifying spectacles of cutting out the hearts of living men and the burning alive of young girls in the name of religious sacrifice. Claiming to right pagan wrongs, the *conquistadores* committed new wrongs in the name of Christianity, but interpreted the laws of the State and of the Church to suit their own desires.

Portugal carried on a lively slave trade with Brazil, her own possession, and despite Spanish laws, regulations and courts of justice, slaves were smuggled into Peru, Chile and other parts of South America.

Intoxicating tales of the New World's fabulous wealth caught fire in Spain, generating a "gold rush" of unscrupulous fortune hunters, men who never dreamed the Spanish dream, men whose only dream was greed and lust for gold.

6. **Ibid.**

Men who were ruled by human passions, cruelty and hate; men who regarded the Cross as a banner, not a creed.

Their brothers, no less physically strong, but invigorated with the power of humility and Christian charity, the black robed Jesuits, the gray robed Franciscans, the white robed Dominicans, consistently dedicated their entire consecrated lives to God and to the service of men. Theirs was the unequivocal principle of human freedom. Forgetful of self, they carried the Faith of the Cross to the heathens of the New World. They endured physical and mental oppression rather than to equivocate the absolute freedom of the men they had come to teach and to keep.

Two Dominican priests from the West Indies cried loudest against slavery. In 1509, Fray Montesino declared that slavery was as criminal as robbery or murder and that slave holders could not receive absolution until they released their slaves. His contemporary, Fray Bartolome Las Casas went even farther.

As a young college student, Bartolome had received an Indian slave as a gift from Columbus, in recognition of his father's participation in the expedition. Isabella, upon learning that Columbus had brought Indian slaves to Spain, promptly sent Bartolome's slave, along with all his companions back to his American home and freedom. Later Bartolome Las Casas, an intimate friend of royalty, set out, as one of the early colonists, for the West Indies, where he became a wealthy man of affairs and an influential political leader.

But at the peak of a successful career, he sacrificed all worldly goods and power to become a priest. Because of his energetic and militant theses, sermons and work to keep the Indians free, he was appointed Bishop of Mexico. In 1539, Las Casas returned to Spain, continued to write and plead against slavery and to advise his king. In 1542, through the influence of Las Casas, Charles V issued the decree which, "absolutely forbade slavery of Indians for any cause." [7] The rights of the natives were definitely and specifically outlined prohibiting forced labor, prohibiting removal from their native dwellings, prohibiting punishment without trial, etc. These specifications became basic to all missionary endeavor. Today, a beautiful statue of Fray Bartolome de Las Casas, the priest who identified himself with the freedom of the Spanish American Indian, stands near the east facade of the great cathedral in Mexico City.

To civilize and to christianize the Indian was the motivating ideal behind the missionary and colonization movement. Yet, spiritual and moral forces met head-on with unrelenting materialism. The arguments were long and bitter and violent. They resulted in scattered civil wars and Peru's eventual separation. In 1713, Spain not only gave up Minorca, Gibraltar and Florida at the Treaty of Utrecht, but signed a a contract (*Asiento*) which gave England exclusive rights to import slaves into all Spanish possessions. Nevertheless, one thing was certain, that the laws of King Charles and the writings of Las Casas determined Spanish policy regarding the Indian of New Spain. The missionaries came to teach, not to massacre or to enslave. The Indian would learn the dignity of work and the resulting reward of independence through individual effort; he would learn the fundamentals of Christian Faith; he would be promoted

7. Clinch, **New Spain**, Vol. 1, p. 61.

from his tradition-bound way of life to one of individual freedom; he would learn the responsibility and the means of self support; he would become oriented into the new era of personal dignity and self-expression.

Without these regulations, without these ideals, missionaries would not have sailed to the new world. To save heathen souls and to assure their freedom was the fundamental ideal of the missionary movement. This was the basic ideal of western civilization and the force that pushed European Christian civilization westward in the New World. Unfortunately, human activity often disregards these ideals, still, like the deep undercurrent of a chafing river, the sustaining spirit of a civilization guides its course through the ages.

Christopher Dawson says, "The religious ideal (of European civilizations) has not been the worship of timeless and changeless perfection, but a spirit that strives to incorporate itself in humanity and to change the world."[8] It was the missionaries' consistent adherence to these principles that caused frequent friction between the men of the cloth and those with political and military authority, but it was the spirit that pushed Christianity westward.

Their purpose was summarized by St. Paul as he spoke to the Corinthians, "We preach not ourselves, but Jesus Christ our Lord and ourselves merely as your servants in Jesus. For God, who commanded light to shine out of darkness, has shone in our hearts, to give enlightenment concerning the knowledge of the glory of God, shining on the face of Christ Jesus. But we carry this treasure in vessels of clay, to show that the abundance of the power is God's

8. Christopher Dawson, **Understanding Europe**, p. 34.

and not ours In all things we suffer tribulation, but we are not distressed; we are not forsaken; we are cast down, but we do not perish" (II Cor 4:5-14).

And in this spirit, on June 1, 1750, ten humble missionaries started out for Sierra Gorda to "incorporate (the Word) in humanity and to change the world."

A few Christian Indian interpreters and guides, a soldier, riding horses and pack mules came down to Mexico City to lead them over the two hundred mile winding, dusty mountainous trail. Most of the missionaries rode, but Serra and Palou chose to walk. At an average of fifteen miles a day, with occasional rests, they made the trip in sixteen days.

Home for Serra and Palou, at the end of a long trying journey, was the dismal, dilapidated wreck of Jalpan, the central mission of the Sierra Gorda group. The natives greeted them joyously, but there was little lasting evidence of previous missionary endeavors.

Hanging as uncertainly as its Christian influences, the little settlement was perched along the hillsides above the Rio de Jalpan, a placid enough stream in June, but most anytime a sudden storm could turn it into a rampaging and flooding torrent. A few large sabinto trees, growing along the river banks, offered shade and a welcome greenish, fresh look. On a flat area, scraped off for the purpose, stood the simple, run-down, adobe church, a friary, a few cane thatched shacks, all dilapidated and grimy. This was the miserable religious center of a thousand Indians, not one of whom had gone to confession or received holy communion during the year.

Enthusiastically and vigorously, the two young priests

met the challenge of their new vocation. We speak of "young" priests here, remembering that when Serra was thinking of leaving the university, he was concerned about being too old. I feel confident that he left in Majorca the maturity of professorship, eminence and the responsibilities that bow the shoulders down with care. The short life-span of 1750, compared to ours, would consider a man old when we would think of him as middle-aged or as still youthful. The average life-span in Mexico, even as late as 1940, was thirty-nine.

As in any era, one's age depends not so much on the number of years he has lived, as upon his physical condition, activity and mental outlook. Actually, Serra was a young, healthy, vigorous thirty-six. The renewal of noviceship, and the hope of starting a new vocation, conditioned him, undoubtedly, to start his new work with the same eagerness and youthful exuberance as a newly ordained priest. Palou was nine years younger than Serra, and the fact that his best friends, both Crespi and Palou, were former pupils, would lead us to assume that Serra was always young in thought and spirit.

They would have to start building both souls and shelters, but the first project was to learn the Pame language. Every Indian dialect was different. Those studied at San Fernando no doubt helped, but Pames spoke something else again, and communication came first. They not only learned to speak the dialect, but translated the catechism, liturgy and other prayers into Pame. Then they settled on a plan of community life.

At sunrise and sunset the mission bells rang out calling everyone to the church. Together, they prayed the Mass and followed other devotions, then there was a brief instruction on Christian doctrine. This was carried out one day in Pame, the next day in Spanish. By learning Spanish, the natives enlarged their sphere of communication and could become an integral part of the country. This was important, as we see today. Two million citizens in parts of Mexico where this program was not introduced, during the mission period, do not speak Spanish, only their own Indian dialect, which has no common idiom with communities of a different tribal heritage. Fifty-two different dialects are spoken in Mexico today.

Serra's sense of the dramatic, his imagination and sense of humor helped him to understand the childlike mind of the Indian. To explain abstract ideas, he would dramatize, motivate, encourage, warn and caution by the simple application to everyday life and problems. And the intimate scenes of our Lord's life and that of his Blessed Mother came alive through pageantry, which the natives themselves could act out. By costume, live figures and the spoken word, the reality and the spirit of the Incarnation, Birth of Jesus, Resurrection, Ascension and other biblical scenes were translated into personal experience, understanding and relationship to their own. Many of these customs are still followed in South America and Mexico.

The Pames learned not only about God, but how to live better and more productive lives. Through their contact with the Moors, who had accumulated knowledge from past civilizations, the Spaniards, especially Majorcans, had advanced beyond the rest of Europe in the study of soils, irrigation practices and other important farming practices. This knowledge the missionaries handed on to the natives of New Spain. They gave them seed, improved varieties of corn, beans, squash and sugar cane plants. They cleared the land, pushing back the wilderness, designed and built irrigation

Mission San Diego de Alcala, Serra's first foundation, though threatened by fire, earthquake and other disasters, has endured. This lovely old structure built in 1808 is located inland from the original site.

and drainage systems and taught them the arts of cultivation. All farming and other activity was on a communal basis, distributing food and other necessities according to needs.

Anticipating the day when the Pames would be on their own as independent parishioners integrated into a mixed society, the *padres* taught them business methods; how to buy, sell, bargain and choose the best outlet for their wares and how to distribute the proceeds. The latter was wisely done under the supervision and guidance of the *padres,* who made certain that all were treated fairly and that a reserve supply was held back against possible crop failure.

The primitive did not readily grasp the importance of providing for the future. One priest made. the disastrous decision that his Indians had advanced sufficiently to take over this chore themselves. The result was empty bins, threatening not only immediate starvation, but future famine, due to the lack of seed for planting next year's crops.

From the proceeds of the crops, Serra bought oxen, cows, bulls, mules, pigs, goats and implements for cultivation and harvesting. Both Serra and Palou worked in the fields beside the natives. It soon became evident Palou had that special organizational ability, which made him an efficient ranch manager. He appointed the most dependable Indians as foremen, while he, himself, would supervise and oversee the projects. Although all the mission land, work and production was on a community basis, they encouraged private enterprise. Those who showed special perseverance were given a piece of land of their own, along with a yoke of oxen, some livestock and seed. Others were rewarded according to their individual merits, with blankets, clothing and trinkets. There was much to learn, but friendly and responsive cooperation with the *padres* led to steady and continuous progress.

Besides better farming methods, they learned to make their own clothing and blankets. The women learned to spin, weave and sew; how to care for the children and adopt habits of cleanliness. Religiously they were growing, too. They enthusiastically responded to the little plays, pantomimes and processions and that the basic truths were penetrating was manifest by the regularity with which increasing numbers received the sacraments. But they needed a church, not just a shelter, where people could meet and hold religious exercises, one that through its beauty would give honor to God and inspiration to his people.

To Serra a church was the consecrated space in that particular locale where God takes up his presence, where his Divine Son is really present in the Blessed Sacrament and where, through this presence, the worldly and heavenly spheres meet and fuse. It was a temple of liturgical theology represented in stone, wood, glass, art and music. It was the outward expression of love and unity, where each individual joins with the community as a unified parish, with the church as a whole and with the entire world, in worship, praise and glorification of Almighty God. And it should represent their ultimate in workmanship and art.

The beautiful edifice in Jalpan stands as a gemlike prototype of those ideals and as a lasting monument to Serra's instincts for building, his artistic good taste and most of all, his loving leadership, hard work and perseverance. There is no doubt that he hired an architect and professional masons, but much of the actual labor was done by the Indians, with Serra working by their side.

When the decision and the plans were firm, Serra asked an Indian boy to ring the bells. Loud and clear, their call penetrated the entire area, summoning the Indians to assem-

ble. They listened attentively as the *padre* told them how
they could build a church, their own church, big enough
for all the people and a beautiful church, one that would
give just glory and joy to God.

The Indians, flattered that the *padre* would be interested
in building a fine church in their Jalpan, enthusiastically
volunteered to work on the project. It took seven years of
hard work to complete. Serra wisely allowed the Indians to
work on the church only when they were not needed in
the fields. They worked as apprentices to the hired masons
and learned and took pride in the skills of carpentry, iron-
working, painting, stone masonry.

The women did their part too. Their knitting, weaving,
stocking making had been perfected to the point of building
up a trade with other communities. They bought cotton
from the outside, spun and wove it into blankets, clothing
and other articles, which they sold. The money from this
trade, they used to pay the hired masons. When the church
was finished they owed nothing; in fact, due to outside donations, they had a reserve in the treasury.

Built of yellowish-brown stone found near by, it is fifty
three yards long and eleven yards wide, with high vaulted
ceiling and adjacent sacristy and chapel. A ninety foot tower,
with rounded openings for the bells, supports a five foot
ornamental iron cross. Reminiscent of the Majorcan-Moorish
influence, the windows are Arabic, otherwise, the design
is classic. The facade is beautifully decorated with statues,
symbolic vines and wheat, all exquisitely and delicately
blended into a delightful pattern. Today, the church at
Jalpan stands much as it was when finished over two hundred
years ago, Spanish charm perpetuating the art, the ideals,
the dreams of Father Junipero Serra.

The other five missions, under the leadership of Serra as president, were developing in varying degrees along the same lines as Jalpan. Each had built a church, but none compared in beauty and elaboration with Santiago de Jalpan. Many of the natives now owned their land and were independent farmers; others were sufficiently skilled to become independent; the granaries were filled; Spanish settlers were coming in and the Indians were becoming a civilized integral part of the growing area. Small Christian towns were springing up in the little valleys and, as in Majorca, their days were regulated by the sound of bells.

But they had their problems. Though the groundwork of establishing Sierra Gorda missions had previously been done, the three Majorcans had tasted their first rigors of missionary life and tested their capacity for self abnegation and control. While most of the Indians were friendly and cooperative, among them were individuals behind whose silent, stoical exterior lurked the hate and distrust of pagan superstitions, hostility and treachery. On one occasion Serra narrowly escaped assassination, and violence was a constant threat. Hunger, filth, stench, sickness, death, the slow mental reactions of primitive minds and the acerbative moods of tough Indians were a way of life. Only a steadfast and profound faith could have sustained them. Yet, avidly, Serra and his companions, with characteristic detachment and renunciation of human comforts, accepted and offered all these things and more in union with the Cross of Christ for the salvation of the souls they had come to teach and direct.

He would "Always go forward; Never turn back." [9] These

9. Tibesar Writings, Vol. 1, p. 3.

words, written to his parents from Cadiz, formulated the firm intention from which he would never deviate; the motto he would follow indefatigably to the end. The eight years at Sierra Gorda had been fruitful. They had followed in principle the missionary system established in New Spain two-hundred years before and the same plan would govern their future missionary endeavors.

The work had been wrought with anguish, frustration and uncertainty, but there were rewards, the greatest of which was the affectionate response of the Indians to his love. He had taught with clarity and patience, reaching out to involve the primitive mind in the comprehension of a purposeful life here on earth and the hope of eternal salvation. Through active participation in the realities and the ritual of the liturgy, they had learned basic truths, prayers and the commandments, the importance of honesty, charity and monogamy. Through the grace of baptism, confirmation and the other sacraments, the Holy Spirit had penetrated their souls endowing many with a deep faith that would live on through successive generations.

A mutual love had developed between the Padre, who had suffered for them, fought for them, lived and worked with them and his faithful subjects. But on September 26, 1758, Serra was called back to San Fernando and regretfully left Sierra Gorda behind. However, when Serra learned what plans they had for him, he was electrified. The Viceroy had asked for four of San Fernando's top missionaries to go to San Saba, the Apache country in Texas, where martyrdom was almost a certainty.

It was critical to the expansion and security of New Spain and the future hope of colonizing California, to open safe inland routes to the north and the west. As early as

1609 missions were established around Santa Fe. There and in New Mexico, for almost one-hundred and fifty years, peaceful missionary life made remarkable progress among the Apaches and other tribes. Father Kino had opened Texas and other northern districts to missions and presidios. In 1760 the fourteen settlements of New Mexico and El Paso had a population exceeding that of the English Colonial Georgia at that time. All was going smoothly until fur traders from Canada and other opportunists stirred up trouble among the Indians. Friendly tribes became barbarous. On fast Arabian horses, brought in by the Spaniards, they galloped over the plains, fighting each other and the Spanish settlers, burned, murdered and raided the fine herds of cattle built up by the missionaries and settlers. They discovered that beef was more palatable than buffalo meat and there was a constant and ready market for stolen livestock among French traders. Individual raids grew into treacherous Indian wars. No mission could survive their murderous attacks and military reprisal fomented treachery. Still missionaries volunteered to work among the savages. Only lack of government funds to support military escort, without which no missionary attempt was permitted, held them back.

In 1740 the Apaches were faced with their own problems. Their ancient enemies, the Comanches around Santa Fe, supplied with French guns, descended on the Apaches with renewed ferocity, raiding, killing and continuously harassing them.

The Apaches approached Spanish authorities for protection, with the usual reply that there were no funds. A wealthy layman, Pedro Romero Torreros, offered to pay the expense if the Spanish government would supply soldiers and missionaries to tame and protect the Apaches. It was a good plan, but Spanish bureaucracy was unconscionably slow. Not until 1756 did the government give its approval. Mission San Saba de la Santa Cruz was established in January of 1757 on the San Saba River and a large contingent of militia was sent to build a presidio for the protection of the mission. But in the early months of 1758, the Comanches staged a murderous raid on the mission, brutally killing and mutilating the priests and practically annihilating the settlement.

The Viceroy decided the raiders should not go unpunished. It was at this time that the call came for four top missionaries to go to San Saba. San Fernando called Serra and Palou, considered their most capable and stalwart missionaries.

But the expedition sent to punish the Comanches was defeated and mercilessly run out of the territory. This discouraged further plans and the whole project bogged down in confusion. It was a severe blow to Serra and to the expansion of New Spain. The Comanches had won a decisive victory (one of many they would win before the successive efforts of Spain and Mexico and finally the military might of America would tame them) and Spain was temporarily denied a land route to the north and the west.

From 1758 to 1767 Serra's headquarters were the College of San Fernando in Mexico City, where he was on call for short missions, Novenas and special sermons in other parts of Mexico. Once again the eloquent speaker charmed congregations with his clear, musical voice, his lively quick wit, ready smile, and fresh wisdom that reached into hearts with love and understanding. A less humble man would have accepted the unsolicited praise, flattery and adulation and comfortably settled down in an aura of eminence and fame. But in the New World, as in Majorca, Serra rejected popu-

1672. Father Serra. The founder of the missions in California is seen with a young Indian convert in the gardens of the Mission San Juan Capistrano, California.

larity and acclaim. He obeyed the orders of his superior and served diligently on all assignments, but he accepted them as training in self-discipline, and spent his free time in prayer and austerities. He ate sparingly and except for a brief afternoon siesta, slept only four hours, spending the rest of the night in prayer and meditation. Between assignments, when in residence at the college, he tenaciously followed the stringent rules for novices and training priests, and devoutly joined in the community prayers and liturgical exercises, growing in divine grace and the simplicity of love.

THE KING." Under this impressive signature Charles III, King of Spain, early in the year 1767, put a sealed secret order to all the Viceroys in his realm. It was one of the extraordinary efforts of history, demanding ingenious methods of secrecy, planning and timing. Travel schedules for all personal couriers were so arranged to assure that each royal document would be delivered into the hands of every Viceroy in each province of the vast empire at approximately the same time, well ahead of the opening date, June 24th. Anyone who opened the document before that date could be punished by death.

On the morning of June 24th, Marquis de Croix, Viceroy of New Spain, as did all deputies on the continent and in the other parts of the New World, read words that shook the world. All Jesuits were to be banished from Spanish soil!

He, the Viceroy, was thereby appointed agent, and was so ordered, in the name of the king, to arrest and deport to the Papal States, every Jesuit now in New Spain. Should one remain in the territory, on completion of the embarkation, though he be incapacitated, ill or dying, the Viceroy would be put to death. No explanations, no reasons were given for this rare, autocratic use of monarchial power over a religious order. For the more than six thousand popularly venerated men, many of whom were of the highest intelligence and personal character in Spain, there would be no recourse, no trial. Discussion, questioning, irresolution would be subject to the death penalty. Obedience must be swift and absolute.

New Spain received the shock of this despotic measure with sheer gravity. Religious orders had given spirit and purpose to the growth, expansion and development of the New World. For almost three hundred years, the zealous Jesuits had courageously and compassionately worked with the natives and settlers, disregarding pain, hunger, disease and death. They had explored the wildest regions; established missions in unknown, barbarous lands; built innumerable colleges, schools, seminaries and magnificent churches. They had brought knowledge, culture and Christianity to the New World.

Why? The unspoken question was on everyone's mind. Charles refused to tell his reasons, but "kept (them) in his royal heart." [1] This was not the first nor the last time Jesuit authority and autocracy had been questioned. Rumors of accumulated wealth had led to dissatisfaction and envy among certain groups. Still, Charles' ban, with its characteristic

1. Clinch, **New Spain,** Vol. 1, p. 182.

sudden finality, could only be classified as an arbitrary exercise of royal prerogative. Charles must have had other than personal reasons.

Whatever spurred the act, there is no doubt that friends of the Jesuits in South America and Mexico regarded the ban as an intolerant and unjust tragedy of history. Still, a "Most Catholic King," [2] Charles III, vehemently upheld and promoted the original Spanish ideal, that their right to colonize and govern the New World was the Spaniard's purpose and capacity to spread western culture and Christianity to the Indian. As did his predecessors, Charles believed that colonial expansion and the missionary movement were inseparable. In this as well as political and economic affairs, he was one of Spain's most successful and popular monarchs at a crucial period in Spanish history.

Regardless of opinion, submission to the royal decree was imperative, as Tennyson later observed of other despotic decrees, "Theirs not to make reply, Theirs not to reason why, Theirs but to do and die." [3] In this case it was to do *or* die. The right man was on hand to carry out the order. Marquis de Croix appointed his good friend, the forceful man of action, Don Jose de Galvez, who had recently come to New Spain as Visator General of the king.

The next morning, every Jesuit institution, in and within marching distance of Mexico City, was surrounded by a military guard. The officer in charge presented and read the royal order to the Father President. As passive instruments of royalty, the soldiers performed their duties in the best orderly and military manner, yet without abandoning human

2. **Ibid.**, p. 190.
3. Alfred Lord Tennyson, **Charge of the Light Brigade** — Stanza II.

understanding. At one monastery the priests were saying their morning Masses when the order was read. The superior asked permission for them to finish. This was granted. Then without protest, each packed his knap-sack, taking only essential personal belongings, and left.

Execution of the order took longer in more remote areas. Baja, (Lower) California, the narrow, far western peninsula, accessible only by crossing the Gulf of California, had no governor. Don Gaspar de Portola, appointed by the king, took office for the explicit purpose of expelling the Jesuits. This was paramount to a doctor removing the heart of the patient he had come to save. The missionaries, catalysts of the meager population of the peninsula, consisting of only about eight thousand still retarded natives, and a scattering of civilians engaged in mining, controlled their political and economic development, as well as their spiritual welfare.

Back in the early colonial days, government officials had refused to support missionary activity there. Despite this negative attitude, the Jesuits founded a mission in 1696. Seventy years later, they had established missions the length of the peninsula and had made sound progress in promoting the Indians from their native condition of dull, stupid pain and misery, inertia, filth and hunger to a self-sustaining life of peace and comparative comfort. It is one of the lamentable consequences of governmental control that all this human benefaction, won by so much blood and suffering, should spasmodically and arbitrarily have been disrupted. In February 1769, the sixteen Jesuit missionaries quietly assembled at Loreto, boarded the *Conception,* and sailed to San Blas, on the western coast of Mexico. Jesuit contribution to the Spanish expansion period had gone into history. And all material possessions of the missions fell into the hands of

Romantic painting by L. Trousset in 1877 catches the spirit of the dedication of the second mission in Alta California at Monterey a century earlier. A major objective of the expedition from Baja California, the event's significance was reflected in the pageantry observed. When news of the founding reached Mexico City, all the church bells in the city rang out the tidings.

the king with Portola appointed to guard, govern, control and protect them.

It is evident that Charles' quarrel was limited to the Jesuits and did not extend to other religious orders. Despite heavy handed methods, both Charles and Galvez were acutely aware that Spain's need for missionaries was extremely critical in the remote areas of the Empire. Galvez was not a man to move with caution. Seemingly impressed with the importance of his position and certainly eager to proceed with the task before him, he ordered San Fernando College to fill the vacancies in Baja with Franciscans.

The Guardian of San Fernando would have appreciated the fine courtesies of consultation and discussion. Always thwarted by a man-shortage, Galvez' order pressed an already tight predicament. Queretaro and Santa Cruz, comparatively new missionary colleges, were equally pressed for men. But by pulling missionaries from Sierra Gorda and reviewing assignments with the other colleges, in the course of a few months, fourteen Franciscans assembled at San Blas for duty in Baja.

Father Serra, who was given a mission at Mesquital, some distance from Mexico City at the time, had no previous knowledge of the enterprise until San Fernando ordered him to go to Baja as President. That he had been ordered to this new post, always gave the zealous missionary joyous assurance that the call had been the will of God and not the consequence of his own solicitation.

After a frustrating period of substitutions, transfers and strenuous traveling, the fourteen Franciscan missionaries, including Serra's special friends and fellow Majorcans, Fathers Palou, Crespi and Raphael Verger, on the 14th of March 1768, boarded the *Conception* and sailed for Loreto.

Blown off course by erratic winds, tossed and buffeted, the little ship, after two weeks, reached the other side of the narrow channel. On Holy Saturday morning, April 2nd, they walked in procession from the beach landing to the church, singing "Salve Regina," a traditional hymn, with a crisp, marching tempo, still sung in Catholic churches: "Hail, Holy Queen, enthroned above, O, Maria! Hail Mother of mercy and of love, O Maria! Triumph, all ye Cherubim, Sing with us ye Seraphim, Heav'n and earth resound the hymn, Salve, Salve, Salve Regina!"

The group celebrated Easter Sunday together at Loreto. After each of the others said a Low Mass, Father Serra sang a solemn High Mass and preached a moving sermon. Then Portola read the Viceroy's letter, legally turning over the missions of the Jesuits to the Franciscans. But contrary to all established missionary procedure and practice, theirs would be spiritual administration of the missions only. All material goods, buildings, furnishings, money and supplies remained the property of the government.

Serra was keenly aware of the problems inherent in such an arrangement. Progress had been particularly slow and disappointing with these primitive natives. Before the Jesuits came the men were completely naked, though the women made a sort of wrap-around for themselves of grasses and animal skins. They gorged when food was accessible and starved the rest of the time. Their diet consisted mostly of roots, herbs, dogs, cats, mice, mule or horse-meat. Fish was abundant along the coast. They were well built, physically agile and brave, but gentle. Not too anxious to work or change old ways, they generally were more concerned with a handout of corn, a blanket or trinket than with the cultivation of a field or the abstract idea of an infinite God. Some acquired new skills, while others were totally incapable of learning. The road to cleanliness, industry and Christianity had been , rough. Government usurpation of mission property could mean the end of the mission movement in Baja California.

Serra had little choice but to acknowledge the letter and promise to conform. His position then, as in future dealings with government officials, was to "Render to Caesar the things that are Caesar's, and to God the things that are God's" (Mt 22:15-21). He would negotiate when possible, but never give in on matters of principle or those which directly affected the spiritual welfare of his subjects. This was a new assignment. He would take no immediate action, but wait for the opportunity to discuss the matter with Galvez, whom he was confident aspired to progressive support of the missions. He issued assignments to twelve of the fathers and they left for their respective posts. Father Parron remained at Loreto with Serra.

Great historical movements echo the aspirations, vision and daring of their leaders; men whose character and fortitude are essential to the fulfillment of dreams. Acknowledged apostle of the California missionary movement was the indomitable and beloved Father Junipero Serra, man of the cloth, spiritual leader, representative of the church, ready and eagerly awaiting doors to open. In this joint effort of church and state, at exactly the right moment, a man appeared whose audacity opened those doors and whose resolution set the whole project afire. Man of the world, representative of the Spanish court, entitled, royally empowered, and newly appointed Visator General of New Spain was the dynamic, intrepid, ambitious Don Gaspar de Galvez.

Son of a poor Spanish farmer, he boasted of noble birth. His father was one of many in Spain whose proud heritage gave him a title, *Hidalgo,* but whose land holdings had been reduced to a small impoverished farm. As a boy, Gaspar worked hard in the fields and with the stock, a life his brothers never left. But at an early age, young Gaspar's outstanding industry and intelligence became apparent to the Bishop of Malaga, who offered to educate him.

Gaspar Galvez lived moderately as an unknown lawyer until his second marriage to a French woman, who knew the right people. His knowledge of French, the language of the court, combined with a felicitous natural grace, a certain attractive, though aggressive personality, — the self-confident and venturesome Galvez rose to the expedient position of secretary to Marquis de Grimaldi, Spanish Minister of State. In 1765, he was sent to New Spain, as Visator General, the king's representative, a title which carried political and military power subject only to the king.

One of Galvez's first duties was to raise funds for Spain. Charles III, a wise monarch, was alert to the problems of the day and dedicated to preserving and strengthening his vulnerable empire. The Golden Age, when Spain was virtually sole master of the western hemisphere and the Pacific Ocean or "Spanish Lake," were but memories. The English historian, F. A. Kirkpatrick, has said, "It may safely be alleged that so vast a region of savagery has never elsewhere been pacified with so much patience and so little violence and that an immense indefensible frontier has never won comparative security at so little cost of life and treasure."

But the world was changing. The age of discovery and conquest had been superseded by the age of trade and colonization. Other European powers with expansion fever cast covetous eyes on Spain's vast domain. French fur traders had advanced down the Mississippi and stirred rebellion among Indian tribes in the North, threatening Santa Fe, New Mexico and Texas. The English colonies' tidal wave was sweeping westward. Spanish Florida had fallen to England. French, Dutch and English trading vessels plied Pacific waters and sought a northern channel across the continent. But what really sent chills down the royal spine was Russian encroachment along the Northern Pacific coast and news of Russian plans to establish colonies on the northern coast of California. Charles III boldly met the challenge of the sixties, the threat to Spain's security, to her prestige, to her progress.

Even before Cabrillo, the sixteenth century writer, Ordonez de Montalva had extolled California's incredible riches. Building the myth, was Cabrillo's discovery of San Diego Bay in 1542 and Vizcaino's glowing description of Monterey Bay in 1602. All Spain quivered at the thought of California, the land of magic and enchantment. All this time the Spanish government had intended to establish missions and presidios there. But Alta California was the far extremity of the western frontier.

Overland routes from Sonora northward and westward had been blocked by great deserts, arid wastelands and recent Indian wars. Manilla galleons and freighters had occasionally skirted the treacherous unmapped California Pacific coast on their way to Acapulco for two hundred years and reported it extremely rough, risky and stormy. To explore and develop the legendary country seemed a wild and unrealistic risk, involving nonsubsistent funds. European wars had drained the Spanish treasury, man power and spirit of adventure

Betty Berg Favello

San Carlos, Carmel, California. The grace of old Spain is wrought by native hands.

and the California enterprise slipped into a Spanish dream. While one-hundred–sixty-seven years glided by, the sun rose over the high Sierras and set in the western sea and no strangers came to taste the beauty and the charm of the fabled far off land.

King Charles, in 1765, sent Galvez to New Spain with specific instructions not only to raise money, but to investigate Russian encroachment in California and the possibility of establishing three missions there, one at San Diego, one at Monterey and another halfway between. Each year the threat became more real. Grimaldi wrote Galvez that the Russian empress was planning further expeditions to the "Pacific coasts of the Americas," with instructions to "observe such attempts as the Russians make there, frustrating them if possible and giving notice of everything to Your Excellency."[4] Added to this was the advice of the Viceroy de Croix leaving to Galvez' discretion "the adoption of any means that he might judge most opportune for realizing the desired purpose of his Majesty."[5]

The cumulative impact of continued warnings indicated an end to Madrid's long deliberation. Galvez, no doubt, envisioned not only a great challenge to Spain in the California project, but an opportunity for self-advancement: the military garrisoning of Spain's western boundaries; the possible discovery of California's fabled wealth; the colonization of a new world of promise and hope and the christianization of the natives there. It would all add up to great reading in Madrid.

In any event we do not question Galvez's sincerity in

4. Bolton, **Palou's New California**, Vol. II, p. 6.
5. Bolton, **Palou's New California**, Vol. I, p. 201.

promoting missionary expansion. He did more than "investigate" and "observe" events in Alta California. Taking the calculated risk that firm orders would follow Grimaldi's warnings, he proceeded to lay plans and organize activity. His was the trump card. Firm orders did come to "occupy" before the plans became operational.

Removal of the Jesuits from Baja missions had given him virtual control of all property, supplies and livestock on the peninsula, plus the vast wealth of gold, silver and pearls he believed the Jesuits had stored there. Assuring his political background, he talked to Marquis de Croix, Viceroy of New Spain and the two leaders agreed it was extremely important to implement the California project with all possible force and haste.

He would have preferred a land passage through Sonora and New Mexico, but due to the Indian wars, the rampaging, wild, savage Indian tribes, plus the merciless desert, expeditions through this route were impossible. Realistically looking to the future, however, Galvez, determined to secure a base of communication through the northwest area, sent a military expedition of over a thousand men under command of General Hugh O'Conor to tame the Upper Pames, Apaches and Comanches. It was no easy task. Painted and screaming, the savages would ride in surprise attack, burning, killing and horribly mutilating their victims. Taming these tribes was a slow and bloody process. In the meantime, Galvez proceeded with the conquest of California by sea.

Convening the wisest and ablest talent in Mexico, ship captains, engineers, masons to discuss the most efficient methods of procedure and fitting their advice together, he gave orders to build a naval base at San Blas. A humid, mosquito infested, shallow harbor, it was strategically located on the west coast of Mexico. Other orders included building two ships and commanding a third. Three ships should be immediately manned, supplied and conditioned for the hazardous voyage up the coast to San Diego and Monterey. Two land parties would proceed from here to the North through Baja and meet the ships at San Diego. Portola would lead the land expeditions and Serra was named President of the missionary project.

Once everything was set in motion, Galvez boarded the *Sinoloa* for Baja. Master of men and affairs on land, the Visator General was helpless before the calm of the gulf. With no favorable wind in her sails, the little ship was forty days in crossing the one-hundred mile wide channel.

Finally, ashore in the southern part of the Baja peninsula at Ensenada de Cerralvo, Galvez lost no time. He wrote Serra of his plans and set up headquarters at Santa Ana, asking Serra to meet him there to discuss details.

At long last the doors had opened! All that Serra had longed for, hoped for, prayed for was now a reality. He gave orders for the mission bells to ring out, proclaiming the joyous news. Then he celebrated a Mass of thanksgiving. While the bells of Loreto were ringing, Serra shared his exaltation with the other Baja missionaries by letter, telling them of Galvez's announcement and suggesting that they too ring the mission bells and offer Masses of thanksgiving.

Serra also wrote to Galvez, congratulating him in the name of all the other Franciscans and stating that he would gladly volunteer his own services "to erect the holy standard of the cross in Monterey" ... to meet the heathen, to "baptize him in the name of Jesus Christ"[6] and to found missions

6. Geiger, **op. cit.**, Vol. I, p. 201.

in the new land. It seemed more than he had dreamed of. Opportunity had come at last, to carry the Cross of Christ to a new land.

In the meantime, Galvez had been inspecting the missions in the vicinity of Santa Ana. What he saw there and later at the other missions astounded and infuriated him. The Baja missions, thriving and prosperous under the Jesuits, now, after a few short months of scandalous military destruction were practically destitute. In order to tighten the grip on the military and salvage what was left, he turned all temporalities over to the missionaries, except at Loreto. It was a sort of dichotomous arrangement, however. The missionaries had more leeway of distribution. They could apportion seed and food to the natives, but each was ordered to make an inventory of all goods on hand with perspective and emphasis on systematic and efficient decisions regarding supplies that could be spared for the Alta California missions.

The Jesuits had dammed the streams, built aqueducts and engineered intricate irrigation systems for the dry, desert-like land. They had found no defense against the devastating hordes of locusts, and harvests were uncertain. Food often had to be transported from one mission to another. Still, the Indians were living well and in good seasons they produced wheat, corn, beans, rice, oranges, bananas and cotton and had stored reserve supplies in warehouses for seed and as insurance against crop failure. Through the years they had built up fine herds of cattle, that roamed and thrived on mission lands.

All was progressing comfortably. Then, with the Jesuits gone and government in control, the soldiers came. They slaughtered hundreds of livestock, stole from the herds, confiscated warehouse reserves and damaged mission property, tore down buildings for the materials and took possession of what was handy.

Investigation attested that the glowing rumors of Jesuit hordes of gold, silver and pearls were just another myth. In the past, Baja was renowned for her pearls, a special type of rare pink jewel, coveted in the courts of Europe. But by 1768, this lucrative business had faded and the pearl beds were practically exhausted.

If Galvez had anticipated reimbursement from the Baja mission property for the large scale spending he had set in motion, this prospect soon faded. But there was the Pius Fund. In the absence of government support for missionary endeavors, the Jesuits had turned to their friends, some of whom were wealthy Spaniards, for donations. These sums of money the fathers had wisely placed in a capital reserve account, using only the interest for missionary purposes. Galvez dipped deeply into this reserve, his justification being that the original purpose of the Fund was specifically set up for advancement of Christianity among the natives.

Undismayed, though angry over his discoveries of military wantonness, Galvez assigned some of the offending soldiers' overseers to active duty in Sonora. Others were signed for service in Alta California. Then he turned to the Franciscans for restoration of order. Though many essential items were lost, he did find a surplus of church goods. These he ordered packed for shipment to the Alta California missions.

Serra's old leg infection had persisted through the years and now, at the critical moment when maximal physical endurance and energy were demanded, it flared into a feverous, intensely painful ulcerous condition. But this did not prevent his traveling to the nearby missions. Accompanied by Palou or one of the other fathers, they examined church

Betty Berg Favello

Wooden spanish gate of Mission San Carlos, Carmel, California.

goods, choosing articles that could be spared for the Alta project. They made arrangements for packing vestments, chalices, candles, ornaments, statues, linens and bells, and for agricultural tools, seeds, plants and grain. No less important were brightly colored cloths, beads and trinkets for presents to the Indians of the new land. In all these endeavors the Baja Indians worked with the *padres,* packing, lugging and transporting the goods from the various missions to La Paz where they were loaded on the ships.

Barely able to walk, Serra could not conceal his condition from Galvez, who fearing the *padre* would delay the expedition, insisted that he give up the long, arduous land journey. But pain and discouragement only whetted Serra's determination to go.

Another thing was bothering him though. The three missions to be founded were already officially named: San Diego de Alcala, San Carlos, at Monterey and San Buenaventura, at an undetermined point. "Is there to be no mission in honor of Our Holy Father St. Francis?" Serra asked Galvez. "Let him find the port bearing his name and he will have his mission there,"[7] is said to be the Visator General's reply.

New energy and new urgency swept the Baja peninsula. Never before had it known the excitement and noise of so much activity. The fever of adventure was in the air. It reached down through the ranks to everyone, reflecting the spirit of the discovery age, electrifying the thrill of opening new territory, that chimerical land of beauty and enchantment, California.

After buffeting capricious Gulf winds, the *San Carlos*

7. **Ibid.**, Vol. I, p. 204.

and *San Antonio,* leaking and listing, limped into La Paz, on the southeast coast of Baja. Both ships were unloaded, careened and repaired. Indians, carpenters, masons, engineers, sailors were all working at high speed. So was Galvez. Besides organizing and checking accumulating supplies, supervising the work of packing and stowing the cargo, he worked beside the workmen, caulking, examining the seams, the masts and the entire structure of the ships. And he urged them on, anticipating winter storms.

Besides fitting and loading the ships for the first expedition, they built warehouses for the accumulation of supplies to maintain the new settlements. La Paz rang with the sharp repetitious beat of the thudding hammers, bumping lumber and the unrelenting screech of saws, while Indians methodically molded adobe blocks, mixed and carried mortar.

Since September, Don Fernando Rivera y Moncada, former Captain in charge of the military unit guarding Loreto, under orders from Galvez, had been traveling northward from mission to mission gathering cattle and supplies for the Alta California project. Serra, reluctant to criticize, remarked that Rivera's orders to gather supplies did not imply a "raid" on the Baja missions. Rivera, evidently, showed little compassion for the survival of the Baja missions in his eagerness to please Galvez. He swept the peninsula missions clean, taking livestock, hay, wheat, corn, horses, mules, Indians and soldiers. In each case, he left a receipt for what he took, but the Baja *padres* complained this did not satisfy hunger nor transfer workers.

Vicent Vila was named captain of the flagship *San Carlos* and head of the sea expeditions. Finally, on January 1769 the *San Carlos* was ready to sail. Packed and sea-worthy, she quartered sixty-two men. Father Hernando Parron, Serra's assistant at Loreto, was named chaplain. Others included Lieutenant Pedro Fages and his twenty-five Catalan leatherjacket soldiers, who had been called back from the Sonora front, Don Miguel Constanzo, an experienced engineer and cosmographer, Dr. Pedro Prat, two blacksmiths, a baker and members of the crew.

Serra's leg was still painful, but it did not prevent his personally going to La Paz for the launching of this great adventure. All members prepared themselves for the expedition by going to confession and receiving the Holy Eucharist. Father Serra sang the High Mass, then the Visator General turned orator. He reminded them that each member was an important individual unit in the occupation and security of California in the name of God, the King and the Viceroy and that their names would be written in history. Indeed, the historical outcome of the venture would largely depend on their conduct. They must keep peace among themselves and among the heathen. They must always show respect and reverence for the chaplain and the other missionaries. Father Serra blessed the assemblage, the flags, the ship and Father Parron knelt for his personal blessing. The little bark then took to the sea. Father Serra returned to Loreto and the California operation was on its way.

About a month later, February 15th, the *San Antonio* set sail for Cape San Lucas at the southern tip of the peninsula. Her captain was Don Juan Perez, a native Majorcan from Palma and seasoned master mariner, who spent many years in the Pacific piloting Manila galleons between the Philippines and Acapulco. Fathers Vizcaino and Gomez were the chaplains. The launching ceremony was much the same, as for the *San Carlos,* but without Father Serra, who was in Loreto, making his own preparations for leaving.

Portola, as efficient an administrator as he was an able military leader and governor, was busily supervising, organizing, equipping and planning the thousand details that would move an expedition army smoothly through rough, unknown territory. His group left Loreto March 9th, and after loading the selected supplies at the various missions, would meet Rivera at Santa Maria, an agreed assembly point for men and supplies and official starting point of the land expeditions from Baja.

Serra spent Holy Week at Loreto. Mule pack trains moved deliberately and he would have no trouble reaching Santa Maria at the appointed time. On Easter Tuesday, (anniversary of the Easter Tuesday he left Petra twenty years before), Serra set out on a broken down mule, one Indian boy helper, a loaf of bread and a piece of cheese. A bit of irony slips into his diary as he sums up his year at Loreto, "all the year I passed there I was only a guest of the Royal Commissary, whose liberality at my parting only extended to the aforesaid bread and cheese." [8] This does not reflect on Portola, whom Serra liked and admired, but indicates the harassing limitations imposed on the Franciscans by the government usurpation of property. He had no home to call his own. "A guest," in the governor's house, he was accepted more as a servant. On his arrival, he had been assigned a bed and a chair in the dining room, a definite limitation of freedom for one in his official position. Evidently, upon leaving, the aging *padre* received the same lack of compassion and concern for his comfort.

8. Tibesar, Vol. I, p. 43.

But others were more thoughtful. He first stopped at Mission San Xavier to see his good friend Palou, who would remain as President of Baja missions. Serra esoterically revived by the surging hope of fulfilling a life-time dream, was still visibly moved by the sadness of parting. Palou shared his friend's joyous aspirations, but he was justifiably worried about the ulcerous leg. Obviously in serious condition, it was robbing the *padre* of his natural physical vigor. Confidentially Palou urged Serra to forego this arduous trip, certain to present untold hazards and hardships that would test the fortitude of the strongest and youngest of men. But his admonitions received the expected firm and simple reply. He had placed all his confidence in God and hoped, "He will grant me (the grace) to reach not only San Diego to raise the standard of the Holy Cross in that port, but also Monterey." [9] Serra's determination was more impregnable at San Xavier than at Cadiz, when he had written his parents he would, "Always go forward and never turn back." [10]

When after three days it was time to leave, the infection had so weakened the missionary that he was unable to mount the mule without the help of two strong men, who literally lifted him and adjusted him into the saddle. Reinforced with supplies of food, clothes and "traveling conveniences" that Palou had thoughtfully packed for his friend's sustenance and comfort, it was time for farewells. Serra, hoping to call Palou to California later said, "Goodbye, Francisco, until we meet in Monterey, where I hope we shall see each other and labor in that vineyard of the Lord." [11]

9. **Ibid.**, p. 66.
10. **Ibid.**
11. **Ibid.**

Francisco's less optimistic farewell was, "Goodbye, Junipero, until eternity." [12]

On his way north, Serra stopped at the various missions to personally select and arrange for church supplies to be shipped to the Alta missions. In each case, the resident priest shared his meager store of flour, corn, figs and raisins with his beloved superior. At Guadalupe, Father Sancho had spotted a bright Indian boy of about fifteen, who could speak Spanish, serve Mass, cook and was generally useful. When he asked his parents for permission to let him go, they proudly agreed to this distinctive privilege for their son. The boy, not only excited about the venture, was elated to be the master of his own mule, a leather jacket and accoutrement duplicating those worn by the soldiers. By now, Serra's supplies had so multiplied from the original loaf of bread and piece of cheese that he required the help of two lively Indian boys to pack and care for the pack animals.

At Santa Gertrudis, Father Donisio Basterra had little to give. Rivera's "heavy hand" had mercilessly and pitifully stripped this poor mission, leaving the *padre* disconsolate and lonely, with no interpreter, no military guard, no assistant, a bare minimum of livestock and a pitifully small group of Indians, mostly old men, women and children. Serra regretfully could offer Basterra only consolation and hopeful promises.

A launch from La Paz, carrying extra supplies for the expedition, was anchored offshore at Santa Maria. Portola's men were busy unloading this cargo and packing it for the mule train when Serra caught up with the expedition. Rivera's group had moved ahead, with the cattle, to Velicata's

12. **Ibid.**

more verdant pasture land. Serra, anxious to get on with the project of the new mission at Velicata, proposed to Portola that they move ahead. As it would take at least another four days for the men to finish the packing, Portola, Serra and Father de Campa, with one soldier and two page boys, moved on ahead of the expedition. They could easily cover in one day the distance the mule train would make in two.

On Pentecost Sunday, they cleaned out a little hut, to serve as chapel and prepared an altar. In his diary Serra tells us, the soldiers "putting on their full accoutrement, leather jackets and shields, and with all the surroundings of holy poverty, I celebrated Mass...consoled with the thought that it was the first of many to be continued in this new mission." [13] He blessed the cross they had erected near by, then officially appointed Father de Campa in charge of the new mission. But no Indians appeared at the founding of Serra's first mission.

All around were footprints indicating a large group of Indians lived in the vicinity, but all ran off and hid. Not until the second day after the founding did they appear. When Serra came out of the improvised chapel after saying Mass and giving his thanksgiving, "thanking His Majesty for the fact that, after so many years of looking forward to it, he now permitted me to be among the pagans in their own country," [14] twelve Indian men and boys stood before him "as naked as Adam in the garden before sin." [15] He filled both their hands with figs and Portola gave them raisins, tobacco leaf and food. The strangers accepted their gifts with friendly appreciation. Then Serra told them, "that the

13. **Ibid.**, p. 71.
14. **Ibid.**, p. 72.
15. **Ibid.**, p. 63.

Father would be their best friend and these gentlemen, the soldiers who are to stay with the Father would do them much good and no harm; that they must not steal the cattle; when in need call the Father." [16]

One day out of Velicata, Serra's leg infection caused so much pain he could neither walk nor stand, threatening realization of all those dire predictions that he would become a stretcher case. Portola, on whose shoulders rested all responsibility for leading the expedition to San Diego, was sympathetic, but practical. He suggested that they were still in familiar territory and Serra could easily turn back now. Serra replied again, as at San Xavier, "I shall not turn back." [17] They could bury him among the gentiles, but he would not turn back.

Fortunately for Serra, the expedition had stopped to rest. Ortega, the scout, had discovered that San Juan de Dios was, as Serra described it, "an agreeable spot, with abundant water, pasture, willows, tules and a smiling sky," [18] a fine place for the livestock to renew their strength before the long push ahead into rough, unknown lands. For the first time, all members of the two land expeditions were together. Serra found joy in the reunion, but his leg showed no sign of healing.

He prayed for relief, that he would not hold the rest back, then asked one of the muleteers, "Son do you know how to prepare a remedy for the wound in my foot and leg?" The muleteer surprised at his sudden promotion to medical practitioner replied, "Why, Father, . . . I am a muleteer; I've healed only the sores of animals." "Well then, son,"

16. **Ibid.**
17. **Ibid.**
18. **Ibid.**

said Serra, "just imagine that I am an animal." [19] The muleteer prepared a poultice of herbs and the next day Serra was so much improved he said Mass and was able to proceed with the group.

The willow shade of San Juan faded into memory as the long, plodding line of mules, horses, cattle and men kicked up clouds of dry, loose, hot sand; the sun beat down with pitiless intensity. But encouraging news brought by courier from Father Campa brightened the day for Serra. Forty-four Indians had come to the new mission at Velicata and asked for baptism. Now he knew that his first mission would be a success.

Day after tiring day, they plodded the hazardous miles of dust and desolation under a scorching desert sun. A land of soft solitude and frightful harshness, of fertile, waterless desert, steep, rocky ravines, "sometimes with the greatest difficulty (we were) climbing up and down hills, without any intermission." They struggled through prickley cactus jungles, ancient palm-tree filled canyons, dry, sandy lakes and sheltered, green fertile valleys. Then the desert gave way to great masses of white, sharp, barren rocks, broken and jagged, forming high percipitous foreboding mountains, which blocked their passage and forced them to turn toward the sea.

The northern section of Baja was more fertile, covered with tall grass, large oak trees, wild grapes and colorful flowers. Serra noted locations suitable for future missions and became ecstatic over the wild roses, "the queen of flowers, the Rose of Castile...blessed be He who created them." [20]

19. **Ibid.**
20. **Ibid.**, p. 105.

But all was not roses. Death had preceded them. "Here we came across the grave of one of the Indians who went on ahead with the Captain (Rivera). His bones were scattered: we collected them and buried them again. Either the gentiles or the wild animals had dug out the grave." [21]

Indians of different temperament appeared along the way. At times some followed peaceably on the crest of the hills above the canyon, then disappeared. One group, actually hostile, confronted them with bows and arrows demanding the Spaniards turn back. They refused to leave. As a warning, mounted soldiers shot twice into the air. At this, they fled. Another group "of a more pleasing character ... very polite" gave them mescal and "laid all their weapons on the ground," then acted out a sort of pantomime war, taking the part of both the attacked and the attacker, giving the Spaniards a good laugh. [22]

At one point "one of the mule drivers discovered a silver mine, which all declare to be very rich," Serra muses and wishes, "May it bring them a fortune." [23] At last, "from a hilltop we saw the West Coast Sea that we had been so anxious to reach. We identified this place with what is called on the maps and sea charts: La Ensenada de Todos Santos." [24] "A small bay of all the Saints," which no doubt is the inlet along the northern coast of Baja where the now popular resort town of Ensenada is located.

The last long difficult miles seemed endless, but the little party of intrepid Iberian pioneers finally reached their primary goal. On the morning of July 1st, from a rise they

21. **Ibid.**, p. 85.
22. **Ibid.**, p. 77.
23. **Ibid.**, p. 97.
24. **Ibid.**, p. 105.

glimpsed the tip of San Diego Bay. Still they must travel five more tedious hours before, from another hilltop, they could see the entire bay and two ships, the *San Carlos* and *San Antonio* at anchor there. The California project had successfully completed its initial objective and Western Christendom had stretched a new frontier. Now, all four expeditions were united. Serra wrote, "It was a day of much rejoicing and merriment for all . . . and (we) gave great thanks to God, who after all, had brought us together there." [25] His dreams and prayers for forty years had been answered.

A new horizon of the Spanish domain had opened, that Christendom might grow and "become the Great Society, a tree in whose branches all nations of the earth might come and lodge." [26]

25. **Ibid.**
26. Arnold J. Toynbee, **A Study of History**, p. 125.

CHAPTER VI
HARBOR FOR ST. FRANCIS

SERRA LOOKED down on the sparkling, blue San Diego Bay. Now an impressive reality of the centuries-old mystical dream, he proclaimed it "truly beautiful to behold" and worthy of the fame attributed to it by Cabrillo in 1542 and again sixty years later by Vizcaino. Snugly locked between two protective land points, she lay peaceful and calm, waiting, still and silent as she had through the long years. And bobbing on the clear, smooth surface, the *San Carlos* and *San Antonio* rode at anchor waiting. Rivera's small land party and the cattle had arrived six weeks earlier. All four expeditions were now united on California soil. But congratulations, friendly reunions, scenic wonders and historical romance soon gave way to sorrow.

Tragedy stalked the little group, now severely conscious of its desperate isolation. The *San Antonio* had successfully made the trip in fifty-five days, but the *San Carlos,* blown off course, south to Panama, was one-hundred-ten days enroute. More serious than adverse winds, however, were leaky water barrels, causing a water shortage that forced them to stop and take on fresh water, which they claimed was impure. Whether due to contaminated water or other causes, the crew developed scurvy and dropped anchor at San Diego practically a ghost ship. *San Antonio's* able bodied men, without hesitation, went to the aid of disabled companions and they too became infected. Everyone praised Dr. Prat for his untiring perseverance and solicitude, but neither kindness nor skill could save the men from this agonizing plague of the sea. When the Portola-Serra expedition arrived, all but five of the *San Carlos* crew were dead and only seven of the *San Antonio* crew had survived.

Serra and the other priests inexorably worked night and day caring for and comforting the sick, giving them extreme unction, saying Requiem Masses and burying the dead. In the absence of the lowly lemon, which grows abundantly over San Diego hillsides today, the Spanish conquest of Califfornia all but failed before it started.

Portola, in conference with Captain Rivera and the other officers, reassessed the situation and agreed the wisest plan was for the *San Antonio,* manned with the surviving sailors, to sail immediately for San Blas and recruit a double crew of men and supplies. Portola and his men, still hale and hearty, could carry on in the fulfillment of the solemn intentions of the expedition and Galvez's orders, by setting out promptly for Monterey.

Accordingly, the *San Antonio* left San Diego July 9th, arriving safely at San Blas, twenty days later. Several of the meager crew succumbed to the disease on the voyage, but Juan Perez, the indomitable master mariner of the Pacific, once more proved his superior seafaring proficiency, grim determination and unswerving loyalty.

Five days after the *San Antonio's* departure from San Diego, Portola, with seventy-four men, including Captain Rivera, Lieutenant Fages, Costanzo, the engineer, Sergeant Ortega, Fathers Crespi, and Gomez, muleteers, a group of Baja Indians and a contingent of Catalan leather jacket soldiers started north in search of the fabled harbor of Monterey.

While this troupe of valiant Iberian explorers laboriously progressed through strange California hills, valleys and along rugged sea coasts, a pitifully small and weakened group waiting at San Diego faced troublesome times. Consisting of Captain Vila, of the *San Carlos,* Corporal Juan Puig, a blacksmith, a carpenter, Dr. Prat, Fathers Serra, Parron and Vizcaino, Serra's two Indian boys, eight Baja Indians, a few sailors, not well enough to sail on the *San Antonio* and eight soldiers, all suffering scurvy, they totaled forty persons, more than one-half of whom were incapacitated.

Despite the staggering holocaust of human misery, preliminary steps were being taken for founding the mission. Essential to the success of every mission were an abundance of water, productive soil and a substantially large group of natives. Even before Portola left, Serra and Crespi had investigated the San Diego River, flowing through the rolling hills down into the bay, and concluded that though but a shallow stream in summer, it appeared to be a continuous and reliable source of water. Although not abundant, it was a water supply. The missionaries, trained in the skills of irrigation engineering, would be able to construct the necessary dams, aqueducts and drainage systems to fulfill human needs and carry on agricultural practices.

Scouting the land, they found it "plentiful and good." [1]
They could envisage the rolling hills pasturing growing herds
of cattle, grain in the deeper soil of the valleys, ripening
and flowing in the breeze, vegetables maturing and fruit trees
blossoming in the spring, hopeful of summer harvest. Large
sycamore, oak, willow and poplar trees testified to the special
fertility of isolated silt deposits, where luxuriated "Castile"
roses, grapevines climbing with abandon high into spreading
trees and wild asparagus sprouting fern-like along the bank
of streams. Acorns supplied an affluent diet for deer, antelope,
and natives. Bear, wolves, coyotes and innumerable small
animals roamed the hills and the air was full of the song of
birds.

It was apparent that the Indians, neither as attractive nor
as promising as the land, would present a problem. With light
brown skin, coarse, black hair, flat features, ill-shapen bodies,
extended bellies and a dragging posture, they appeared sloven-
ly, stupid and hostile. Attempting an illusion of lustrous
splendor, both men and women painted their faces. Entirely
naked, the men hung crude ornaments of sea shell from
pierced ears and noses. The women, however, kept decently
covered with reed skirts and tunics of animal skins.

That they were dirty and lazy was no surprise, what
the Spaniards could not abide was their exasperating habit
of stealing. Sly, greedy, tricky and covetous, they stole everything left unguarded, convincing the Spaniards the devil was
in them.

But Serra intuitively saw them only as souls to be saved.
He wrote to Father Andres, Guardian of San Fernando, "Al-

---

1. Serra's letter to Fray Andres, 7-3-1769, Tibesar, p. 137.

Betty Berg Favello

Mission San Carlos Borromeo de Carmelo, founded and built by Father
Serra in 1770 and his headquarters until his death in 1784.

ready God, our Lord has placed into the hands of the holy college (San Fernando) this most abundant harvest.... May God give them and us his holy grace, so that in a short time all will become Christians."[2] Only a heart consumed with the fire of faith and impelled by a consuming love could project their conversion as children of God. To this persistence of dynamic purpose, Western civilization owes its strength.

Despite all obstacles, two days after the bustle and confusion of Portola's departure, on the morning of July 16, Serra founded Mission San Diego de Alcala, the first of the Alta California missions and actually the first of Serra's own. Velicata would fall to the jurisdiction of others, but San Diego was and would be Serra's responsibility — the realization of a spiritual dream — a new mission in new lands, among pagans who seemingly had had no previous contact with anything relating to Christianity, and whose appearance would tend to belie any hope of future acceptance of God or the civilizing influence of men.

On top of the hill, now known as Presidio Hill, overlooking the bay, the able bodied men set up a few small grass huts for shelter. The largest of these, in which they erected an altar, qualified as a temporary church. Here, on that July morning, commemorating Our Lady of Mount Carmel and the anniversary of the historically famous Spanish victory in 1212 over Mohammed, Father Serra said the Mass. Then he blessed and dedicated the large wooden cross erected in front of the church, signifying the purpose and location of a mission. The Cross of Christ now officially blessed and

2. **Ibid.**

planted on California soil, Serra ardently prayed for the salvation of those intractable pagan souls he hoped the grace of God would eventually enlighten.

But the Indians he longed to reach had neither witnessed the proceedings nor the spirit of the ceremony. They hid out. One cause of trouble from the first was the language barrier. Serra had gone to great lengths to bring Baja Indians as interpreters, hoping they might find basic language similarities with the Alta California Indians. But the San Diego dialect had no similarity to any Baja dialect, nor to any other known dialect of New Spain.

It is a strange phenomenon that in California alone the Indians spoke over one-hundred separate dialects, in which there was little or no mutual understanding. These dialects formed eighteen major languages which in turn, fit into six separate language families having no common relationship or origin. Consequently, both Indian and Spaniard were limited to sign communication.

The friendship of one young boy offered a slim hope of spanning this gap. From the least hostile of the different villages or groups into which the natives were divided, came a boy about the age of Serra's Baja page boys, who not only showed every indication of wanting to be friendly, but a lively curiosity for learning Spanish words. Through this association began a code of intercommunication.

Despite this fragile link, day by day the Indians became more unfriendly and malicious. They came regularly to the mission and the camps, accepted gifts, but always with snarling insistence they be given more or some other article that appealed to them. They would wander into the infirmary, ridicule the patients, pull the sheets and blankets off the beds and at the first unguarded moment, run off with them. In desperation, the soldiers would shoot into the air to frighten them off. Unimpressed, they would mimick the soldiers, dancing around crazily and yelling "Bang! Bang!"

All in all, the first months at San Diego were long, agonizing and frustrating. Until the mood of the natives changed, missionary activity stood still. As they waited anxiously for news from Portola and for the arrival of another ship, the misery, suffering and horror of scurvy, its rotting gums, falling teeth, swollen, scarred, useless limbs and slow, painful, helpless death continued day and night. Both Father Serra and Father Vizcaino became infected with the plague, but recovered with no serious consequences. It was a time of constant trial, but Serra heroically endured all hardships, accepting them as sacrificial foundation of the missionary endeavor; the Cross before the Resurrection.

And matters grew worse. On August 15, with characteristic, sneaky cunning, the Indians chose a propitious moment, a moment of changing the guard, when only a minimum number of Spaniards were at the camp. While the men were on their way between the camp and the ship, twenty natives, armed with bows and arrows, attacked the mission.

A miniature battle ensued. Four armed Spaniards fought them off, but Indian arrows found their mark. Three Spaniards, including Father Vizcaino were wounded. The tragedy of the day, however, was the loss of Serra's beloved and faithful Baja Indian boy, the one who had come all the way with him from Loreto. An arrow pierced his neck and he ran bleeding to Serra. "Father, absolve me, the Indians have killed me."[3] He died at Serra's feet in a pool of blood,

3. Maynard Geiger, **Palou's Life of Fr. Serra**, p. 77.

but with the blessing and absolution of the Apostle of California.

Three natives were killed and several others wounded. They had learned the painful and mortal bite of Spanish guns and grew more respectful. Dr. Prat cared for the Indians, as he did for the Spaniards, dressing their wounds and nursing them back to health. His gentleness contributed to a more amenable attitude, at least for a time.

Serra had always resisted any kind of wall or barrier separating the mission from the natives. After this brawl, however, he submitted to the soldiers' insistence on building a stockade around the buildings and keeping the Indians out.

Months wore on. The young San Diego Indian boy, undisturbed by hostilities, continued to visit the Spanish camp and to ask questions. His growing knowledge of Spanish words and reciprocal exchange of native expressions opened wider avenues of understanding and friendship. Soon he was carrying messages to his people, explaining the Spaniards' purpose here and their peaceful intentions. From this contact, Serra not only built a basic vocabulary, but was able to establish perceptive communication and to relate to his would-be converts.

The old year slipped into the new and about noon on the 24th of January, 1770, someone spotted Portola's men coming home. Haggard, dirty, half starved, and smelling of mule, all seventy-four hardened explorers struggled into camp grateful to be back alive, but they had disappointing news. There was no Monterey Bay! They had discovered a magnificent bay, farther north, a harbor large enough to hold the ships of Europe. But nothing they had seen fitted Vizcaino's "O" shaped, sheltered Bay of Monterey.

A thorough examination of the Monterey area revealed

a "grand ensenada or open bay"[4] that stretched out before them between two points, but not matching Bueno's "fine port between which and the river there is a forest of pine trees more than two leagues across,"[5] nor Bueno's Point Ano Nuevo and Point Pinos de Monterey. Bueno had specifically noted that they were of exceptional quality for repairing "masts and spars" and the Portola party rated the pines as "dilapidated"[6] and not suitable for that purpose.

The real sticking point was the differential in latitude. Rivera and Costanzo had made repeated calculations, but the landsmen's reconings would not match the latitude of the exacting seaman, Bueno's ancient chart, nor by any stretch of their imaginations, would the "open Bay" before them correspond to Bueno's sheltered, deep harbor in the shape of a large "O." Bueno had sketched a specific mariner's view, stating a specific geographical phenomenon, location and shape, which did not conform to the findings of Rivera, the landsman and the others. They found Carmel Bay, "a small bight" (a body of water bounded by a curving shore) and the Carmel River "flowing down from the mountains," south of the questionable "open bay," but concluded Monterey Bay must be farther north.

Weather, undoubtedly, was a determining factor in this historical moment of confusion. Clouds of fog may well have obliterated a portion of the headlands. Wind could have ruffled the water, making it appear as a part of the sea.

Whatever the reasons, it is one of those unexplained mysteries of history. Perhaps, as Serra believed, it was God's will and the intercession of St. Francis, that forced these

---

4. Fr. Zephrin Englehardt, **Mission San Carlos Borremeo**.
5. Walsh, **Mission Bells of California**, p. 21.
6. **Ibid**.

"doubting Thomases" to go to the north, where, on October 31, 1769, the Spanish commander, Portola, in full military regalia and large, plumed hat, along with Sergeant Ortega looked down on and discovered the magnificent San Francisco Bay, securely locked in and protected by the narrow "Golden Gate."

They knew now they were north of Monterey and that though they had found a great port, no doubt surpassing that of Monterey, they had been unsuccessful in their mission. Discouraged, starving and physically exhausted, they decided to return to San Diego.

"On Sunday, December 10th, we both (Fathers Crespi and Gomez) celebrated Holy Mass, and everyone attended. Before we departed, a large cross framed for that purpose, was raised on a hillock near Carmelo Bay. On the cross were carved the words, "Dig at the base and thou wilt find a writing!" The "writing" was a full detailed statement of the findings of the first Portola expedition available for all who might follow.[7]

According to plans, the *San Antonio* was expected to meet Portola's expedition at Monterey. Well aware of the uncertainty of sailing ships, they left the "writing," should a ship arrive after they left. Then they trudged back to San Diego. Some of the men became infected with scurvy along the way, but all recovered. On the same day that Crespi mentions the illness of several of the men, he speaks of finding wild berries and is relieved to report that all recovered the next day. There is no doubt that this source of fresh fruit, plus a hunter's contribution of fresh bear, antelope and deer meat did save their lives, along with water cress and

7. Crespi's Diary.

other natural foods. Still the association did not become a fact of medical or natural science for many years to come.

Time was running out at home base. Practically devoid of food, supplies and patience, they could offer the travelers little sustenance. The joy of reunion once more was marred by the gnawing pangs of anguish. San Diego supplies, strained further by the arrival of Portola's seventy-four hungry men, could not last long. Surpassing the ordeal of deprivation was the interminable stench and misery of scurvy, and lingering over all was the ever present threat and the tragedy of death. During Portola's absence, nineteen more men had been buried in California soil.

They were learning to eat Indian food, to fish and hunt. But these were not their sixteenth century forebearers, who had conquered a new world in less than a century, nor were they the nineteenth century frontiersmen who would push America westward. The average eighteenth century Spanish soldier, fresh from a comfortable Catalonian farm or town was hardy, brave, a true loyal patriot, an able fighter, but he was trained in military regulations and maneuvers. Not a forager, he depended on stores from the civilized world, flour, chocolate, beef, shoes, clothes and shelter.

Hope was waning for the help that should have come. The *San Jose* was long overdue. The *San Antonio* should soon return. In the event that either should have by-passed San Diego, Portola could testify that they had not appeared in the vicinity of Monterey.

Had they known what they, no doubt, suspected regarding the fate of the *San Jose,* discouragement could indeed have terminated the enterprise. On her voyage north she had run into head winds and was blown back to Acapulco, from which she had made repairs and sailed again into oblivion.

With her, besides her captain and other personnel, went a carefully selected invaluable cargo, including richly embroidered vestments, altar cloths, statues and gold and silver altar vessels. No trace of her was ever found. Sea support of the California expedition had been practically a disaster, due to the high, cumbersome, tub-like Spanish ships, the awkward square sails, the contemporary lack of nautical tacking and medical defense against scurvy.

Early in February, Captain Rivera with twenty soldiers, three muleteers and Father Vizcaino, who had not fully recovered from his Indian battle scars, left for Velicata to bring back cattle and supplies. The experienced and efficient Rivera would spur on with all possible speed, but a cattle drive over the rugged Baja terrain between Velicata and San Diego would take time. Even the most optimistic calculations could not estimate that the dwindling supplies at San Diego would hold out until his return.

The premises were as clear as a blackboard chart. The conclusion left but one recourse. There was no need of further evidence to prove Portola's loyalty and devotion to the project, but he was not about to sit there and subject the entire assemblage to slow death by starvation. He told Serra he had decided to return with his men to La Paz.

Serra, too, a practical man, could see the logic of Portola's decision, but he was dedicated to a dream, a spiritual dream that would not die. He knew that once Portola and his men left San Diego, the California project was doomed. He pleaded with Portola and prayed to his God. And confirming his stand, he made a pact with Father Crespi that, come what may, neither would go back. The two intrepid priests had an ally in Captain Vila of the *San Carlos*, who was equally determined never to abandon his ship.

Persistent, persuasive and confident enough in Divine
Providence to make a spiritual gamble, Serra induced Portola to agree to a plan. Beginning March 10th, Serra would
conduct a Novena to St. Joseph, patron saint of the expedition.
If help did not come by the 19th, Portola and his men would
be free to leave.

The fate of California's missions hung on the outcome
of those nine days. Serra began the Novena. Everyone participated. But none prayed as fervently as Serra. All his
hope, his love, his faith poured beseechingly to heaven im-
ploring Almighty God, his Divine Son, the Holy Mother,
St. Joseph and all the saints to send help; to save the missions;
to allow the light of truth to be brought to the thousands of
souls who lived in darkness in this beautiful land. All day
he prayed and most of every night. Yet each day it was the
same.

The sun rose over the green hills and set in the changeless, plangent sea. Each day they watched from Presidio
Hill and searching from horizon to horizon saw only the
empty, blue, flat, endless sea. The morning of the 19th was
the same. All received Holy Communion and the Novena
was over. Still there was no sign of a ship. Then at three
o'clock that afternoon, someone called out, "Sail!" All looked
out and from Presidio Hill they could see a white speck rising above the horizon. Like a phantom, off in the distance,
it appeared again, then vanished. There was no mistake,
no illusion. All knew it was a sail. They could not know
if it would return. Now, Portola could not leave.

It was the *San Antonio*. Under orders to sail to Monterey,
she was bound northward, when they had glimpsed her sails.
A short time after they spotted her, she ran into trouble

and stopped in the Santa Barbara Channel. The friendly Indians there came out in small boats to greet the Spanish ship. By means of signs they told Perez that Portola's expedition had returned to San Diego. Perez quickly comprehended the situation and gave orders to turn back at full sail. Three days later the *San Antonio* dropped anchor in San Diego Bay and the California project was saved.

With fresh men, abundant supplies and new hope, Portola promptly made arrangements for the second land expedition to leave for Monterey. Supplies needed for his foray and those required at San Diego were loaded. Everything else remained stored aboard the *San Antonio,* which would sail for Monterey and a rendezvous with Portola.

The first expedition had netted for Portola and the others valuable experience and knowledge. For one thing, they had established the fact that the Indians north of San Diego were friendly and peaceful and that no formidable protective army was needed. On this trip Portola would take only half the number of men and supplies of the first expedition. This would appreciably lighten their burden and speed progress. Portola, his servant boy, Lieutenant Fages, Constanzo, the indispensable engineer, five Baja Indians and Father Crespi, chaplain and diarist, made up the experienced and seasoned group of explorers.

Sergeant Jose Francisco Ortega with eight soldiers would remain to protect San Diego along with twelve Baja Indians, Fathers Parron and Gomez and the faithful Captain Vila, who would rather die than abandon his crewless ship.

All personnel of both contingents attended Mass at San Diego on Easter Sunday. It was their last reunion. The next morning Captain Perez weighed anchor and the *San*

Antonio, with Father Serra aboard, set sail for Monterey. Portola's expedition left the following day, April 17, 1770.

The second trip was a smooth revisitation of familiar territory and amiable people. It was manifest that the first expedition had left a most favorable impression, for on their return, the natives welcomed them as friends. Father Crespi, ever thinking of possible mission sights, had noted on the first expedition, as they traveled along the Los Angeles River, "This plain where the river runs is very extensive. It has good land for planting all kinds of grain and seeds and is the most suitable site of all that we have seen for a mission, for it has all the requisites for a large settlement."[8]

But the Santa Barbara reports were still more glowing. The Indians there were well built, intelligent and had developed a fairly good civilization. They lived in towns of five-hundred to one-thousand people, built thatched roofed houses and carved out skillfully constructed wooden canoes, provided with smoke holes in the center of a cabin and sturdy enough for deep water tuna fishing. Signs, now an accepted language, told the Spaniards that enemies from the mountains would periodically stage violent raids, burning and destroying their huts and villages.

Only thirty-eight days after leaving San Diego, on Ascension Day, May 14, 1770, Portola's party arrived at Monterey, all in good health. The sea was empty of ship or sail. Portola, Crespi and a small military guard went directly to the scene of the cross they had erected near Carmel on the

---

8. Crespi's Diary, Aug. 2, 1769, **Palou's New California**, VII. (Dr. H. E. Bolton, who one-hundred-fifty years later, fully retraced every mile of Father Crespi's travels, states this is the present site of the city of Los Angeles).

last trip. It stood just as they had left it, except that it was arrayed with gifts. Arrows and feathers were carefully placed around the base and strings of sardines and dried meat hung from the arms, but no Indians could be seen. Accepting this as a sign of good will, the Spaniards concluded the Indians were shy, but friendly. Then they pushed on with the task of locating elusive Monterey Bay.

First, they explored from the look-out-points on the hills above the sea. Below them, clearly and unmistakably, lay the large "O" shaped bay, sheltered by the Point of Pines on one side and the Point Ano Nuevo on the other. It was the picture they had expected to find the last time, matching in detail the words of Bueno: a harbor, smooth as a lake with the Pacific Ocean beyond. Large schools of seals, splash-ed and played in the placid blue water. The subsequent discovery of San Francisco Bay had defined the location of Monterey as south of San Francisco and consequently con-ceded the "open bay" they had seen to be Monterey, but as they reasoned, changed by time.

Why was the picture so unmistakably clear now, when it had been so mysteriously obscure before? This is a question that has been asked innumerable times in the last two hundred years. Many explanations of Portola's dilemma have been offered. One is the differential in latitude. Actually, when Viscaino's ship sailed into Monterey Bay in 1602, she was in trouble. Disabled and desperately in need of repair, the little harbor was a welcome anchorage. Bueno's gratitude may explain his exaggerated account of Monterey Bay as the sheltered harbor the realistic explorers of one-hundred-sixty-seven years later failed to recognize.

Furthermore, as everyone who is familiar with the Monterey-Carmel area knows, the changing, shifting winds, drifting mists and fog, can completely change the aspect of the same view seen on a clear and sunny day.

It would only be natural, too, that over campfires in those long, lonely nights at San Diego, they would have kept probing for the answers. Deliberate discussions between land explorers and men of the sea could have mentally reconstructed all factors and Captain Vila might well have advanced helpful nautical observations. All this, no doubt, had resulted in removing practically all indecision and adopted the fact that their "open bay" must truly be Vizcaino's Monterey, even before Portola left on the second excursion. In any event, Portola's second party stood on the hill and beheld the harbor, gloriously blue, calm, sparkling, and just as Bueno had described, in the shape of a large "O." All mystery and doubt were dissolved. Monterey Bay was indeed a reality.

Portola's group set up camp at Carmel, which they had found before to be a more suitable campsite, well protected and with a constant supply of fresh water. Through millenniums, the Indians, too, had selected this as the most favorable area for their home grounds. No sooner had the Spaniards established camp, then the natives appeared with gifts of seeds and venison, their prize possessions. It was clearly indicated that the mutual exchange of gifts and sign communication was leading to a comfortable association.

With little to do but wait, the days passed slowly. At the end of a week, a sail rose over the horizon. As previously agreed, the landsmen signaled their presence by setting three fires and the *San Antonio* acknowledged with canon salvos. Perez evidently found Bueno's nautical directions faultless, for without incident, the little packet-boat entered

Monterey Bay and dropped anchor. The following day, launches took Crespi, Portola and others aboard to celebrate the culmination of another successful step in the California project, greet friends and make plans for establishing the second California mission.

The story of California's missions is rich in spectacular moments. One perhaps surpasses in melodrama, however, that Pentecost Sunday, 1770, when Mission San Carlos de Borremeo was established.

In 1602, when Vizcaino had entered the harbor, aboard were three Carmelite Fathers, Fray Antonio de la Ascension, Fray Andres de la Asumcion, Fray Thomas de Aquino, chaplains of the expedition. They had gone ashore and said the Mass. Bueno minutely described their location under a great oak tree beside Monterey Bay. Portola's party had no difficulty finding the same tree, down by the beach, near a ravine, "whose branches bathe in the sea at high tide."

Here, on the same spot, one-hundred-sixty-eight years later, Portola's men set up a small altar. All members of the land and sea expeditions assembled, leather jacketed soldiers, white bloused sailors, plume hatted Portola and black haired Baja Indian boys. Bells hung from the tree rang out across the bay and reverberated through the hills breaking the silence of nearly two centuries. Strangers heard and wondered, but did not appear.

Serra blessed the large, crude cross, which the men had hewn from timber near by. Serra wrote, "We all assisted in raising it and I blessed it, chanting the prayers of benediction. Then we planted it in the ground and all of us venerated it with all the tenderness of our hearts. With holy water I blessed those fields. Thus with the standard of the King of Heaven raised, the standards of our Catholic monarch were also set up, the one ceremony being accompanied by shouts of 'Long live the Faith!' and the other by 'Long live the King!' Added to this was the clangor of cannonading from the back." [9]

Then Serra sang the Mass, "All the while there was cannonading," and they closed the ceremonies by singing "Salve Regina." [10]

Serra's second California mission was established. The religious ceremonies completed, the rough shod, imperious Fages, geared up for action, plunged into the business of building construction with a vengeance. Costanzo, the engineer, assisted in selecting sites for the presidio and mission and drew the plans. Portola's camp was moved to Monterey, the scene of operations. All agreed that Serra and Crespi would be more comfortable aboard the *San Antonio* until their quarters were available.

The soldiers were put to work. They unloaded the *San Antonio's* cargo, cut lumber, and performed all the tasks of construction.

Her work accomplished, the *San Antonio* sailed out of Monterey harbor July 9, 1770, exactly one year from the day she had sailed from San Diego on her first rescue mission, back to San Blas. With her went Serra's letter to Galvez, describing the joyous ceremonies on the occasion of the establishment of San Carlos mission on Pentecost and graciously thanking the Visator General for the beautiful statue of Mary Most Holy, "which gave this wilderness a look of pious elegance." [11] Upon receipt of this letter, Galvez asked

9. Tibesar, p. 169.
10. **Ibid.**
11. **Ibid.**, p. 185.

Betty Berg Favello

Footsteps through the ages. Old stone steps of Mission San Carlos at Carmel, California.

that all the bells in Mexico City ring in joyous celebration
of the good news that at long last the first two California
missions were successfully established and the Spanish frontier was secure.

Serra wrote Fray Andres, Guardian of San Fernando,
also, asking for more priests, warning that it would not be
easy. Once before in San Diego, he had written, "To sum
up, those who are to come here as ministers should not
imagine that they come for any other purpose than to put
up with hardships for the love of God and the salvation of
souls.... The distances are great...communication by sea
makes it necessary that they endure.... But to a willing
heart all is sweet, *'amanti suave est'* " [12] And again from Monterey, he remained the guardian general, "Hardships they will
have to face — these men who come to sacrifice themselves in
so holy an enterprise — as everyone knows." [13]

Besides Serra's letters, aboard the *San Antonio* were
Costanzo and Portola. The first governor of California, explorer, discoverer of San Francisco Bay, Portola will ever
be revered by Californians for his ingenious leadership and
indomitable courage. Straightforward and unflinching, intelligent and practical, with a full measure of vision and
foresight, he could quickly perceive all aspects of a situation
and acted with discerning wisdom and dispatch. And combined with the superior complexities of leadership, were the
simplicities of compassion that won the affection and respect
of his men and all who worked with him. Especially important to the California project, was his understanding kindness and generosity which won and established the friendship

12. **Ibid.**, p. 139.
13. **Ibid.**, p. 173.

and good will of the natives, a potent psychological victory for the missionary endeavor. We bid him farewell on this last trip with admiration and affection, regretting that he had not remained longer in California to further guide the missionary movement.

The sails of the *San Antonio* slipped away and disappeared over the horizon. Left in Monterey, this last far western boundary of the Spanish Empire, were forty men. Almost a year of anxious waiting lay ahead before they would again receive supplies or have any contact with the civilized world.

CHAPTER VII
BUILDING, PLANNING AND
FRUSTRATION

*B*EFORE BOARDING the *San Antonio,*
Portola warned Fages that under all circumstances he, as
military commander, must remember that the primary purpose of the Alta California conquest was to extend the faith.
The Cross must precede the flag. This balanced and saga-
cious advice, the insensate Fages was lamentably incapable
of embracing.

Fages was strictly a military man: a career man. As military commander he now had power; power he had never before thought obtainable. His new titles "Commander in Chief"
and "Representative of the King" resounded with status, no-
bility. But if the lieutenant appraised his new titles with
awe, he more realistically evaluated his responsibilities with
fear.

Of immediate concern was the constant probability of
a major outbreak among the thousands of savages surround-

ing them. He was awesomely aware that his pitifully small military unit would be totally incapable of handling such a disturbance. Equally frightening was the remote, but, nevertheless, uncomfortably real threat of foreign invasion. And overriding all else, was the ominous certainty that his own personal career hinged on so fragile a basis.

Unfortunately, absorption in this limited outlook precluded a greater vision. Fages could not perceive that his coveted advancement would be determined by the success of the California project, and that both his career and advancement actually rested on the overall administrative policy of friendly cooperation with the Franciscan missionaries.

For all his apprehension, Fages was enterprising, energetic, strong willed and an autocratic driver. His first task was to provide shelter for the little group newly arrived on foreign shores. He ordered the men to work with as much drive and bravado as he would have sent them into battle. Soldier and sailor turned carpenter and mason, working from sunrise to sunset every day of the week. There was nothing like a dose of solid work to keep their minds occupied, the commander theorized. Everyone worked, the priests, the Indian boys, the muleteers. The ring of axe and screech of hammers echoed and re-echoed through pine forests and rose above the distant, but ever present roar of surf. Buildings took shape, enclosed by a heavy, high protective, pine log stockade.

Fages, Dr. Prat and the military personnel lived in the presidio, or main oblong building. The other building served two purposes. The largest section was used for storing reserve supplies and the rest was divided into a palisade of separate rooms, which due to Fages' idiosyncrasies, proved to be something of a jail. The lieutenant, whom Serra called a "ridiculous little fellow," insisted upon keeping the keys to their cells, so he could "lock us in and out when he pleased." [1]

Serra was amused by these minor personal inconveniences. Still as he reflected on the mood of the fledgling camp, he saw growing indications of problems and dilemmas. Fages, an ordinary little man, a good first sergeant, had been given authority far above his capacity. He had driven the men too hard. They were complaining to Serra. He pled their case, and was practically told to mind his own business. Tempers and resentment rose. The men were on the verge of rebellion. Serra saw the irony of the situation. Once the immediate task was completed, Fages would turn them all loose to loiter and roam at will. Lack of orderly, planned military discipline would disrupt the harmonious climate essential for progress.

The more serious and real concern to Serra, however, was that with Portola gone, Fages showed every indication of assuming autocratic control of the missionaries and the missions. This was contrary to the intent of the project and in direct opposition to military orders.

Spanish bureaucracy left ample room for conflict in authority between religious and civil authorities. Regulations clearly specified that the military should not interfere with the work of the missionaries. Conversely, the missionaries had no control of the military. Confusion, frustration and friction was inevitable. Basically, the military were there to conquer. The missionaries were there to teach. Idealistically the government, represented by the military and the Church, represented by the missionaries, were of one mind, pursuing one goal.

1. Geiger, **op. cit.**, Vol. I, p. 279.

The only recourse was the voice of authority and mediation, the Viceroy in far off Mexico City.

Serra resolved to avoid confrontation if possible, and looked with pride and gratitude on the actual foundation of a mission in elusive Monterey.

By now he had seen enough of California to know that it was truly a land of compelling wonderment. Vast and free, it lay unrestricted by pomp and panoply, solemn in its silent, propitious promise. The surging, restless sea, the great, towering snow-capped mountains, the land; the rich, fertile land, burgeoning with life-sustaining wealth, waited. How long it had been waiting, no one knew, but soon now, men would come. They would overflow the land, stir the soil, build, teach, grow, multiply. It all made NOW singularly urgent. This brief interim of time had been opened to them. It soon would pass. This was the moment preserved in history for teaching these poor, delitescent people; a time of preparation of becoming strong in their new found freedom and independence; before they would become absorbed into a pluralistic society.

Serra's spirit, aspirations, imagination and zeal rose to heights he had never known before. He envisioned missions the full length of California ... from Loreto to San Francisco, with a day's travel between. Certainly, it was the wishful thinking of a man of vision. Genius, it might be called in the scientific world; sanctity, perhaps, in the spiritual world. Serra's visions, however, were not outside the realm of possibility, implying cooperation of the military and others involved.

Actually, Serra's "vision" was no illusion. His was the only practical plan that would work. Two feeble missions separated by four-hundred miles of wilderness had no hope of survival. They had made progress in California, but the victory was not yet won. Ominously without infused purpose and drive the entire project faced disaster. Only the solidarity of a well connected chain of productive units could make any impression on the thousands of natives. The same cooperative awareness was essential in facing internal strife or foreign invasion. In Serra's Majorcan heritage there was no room for fear — only straight-forward, hard work to get the job done. Face the problem and tackle it day by day.

In a confidential burst of reckless enthusiasm, and relying on the mutual vision of a friendship in which both understood the same language of boundless love, the love of eternity, he had written to Fray Andres, Guardian of San Fernando. He could use a hundred missionaries!

But the complexity of interwoven governmental and church relationship through which he must work, was definitely bound by hard irretractable, limitations of vision, the limitation of goods, the limitation of fear. Serra's dream was subject to the restraining walls of all these.

In the inmeasurable time it took letters from California to reach their Mexican destination, Fray Andres had been replaced by Fray Raphael Verger, Serra's friend, fellow Majorcan, the very man, in fact, who had burst into Palou's cell back in Palma, with news that one of their own was planning to go to the New World as a missionary. Father Verger was a dedicated Franciscan, devout and sympathetic to the missionary ideal. But Verger was strictly and sedately a conservative man of facts, dates and figures. "One hundred men!" "The man must be out of his mind!" This was Verger's reaction to Serra's letter.

Galvez, Serra's political counterpart with regard to welfare of the missions, was still in Mexico City. In the two years since he had launched the project, his enthusiasm, vision and zeal had remained constant but his diplomacy had grown even more blunt and crude. He contacted San Fernando. Forty-nine missionaries had just arrived from Spain, new, eager, but green. Galvez requested Verger to send all forty-nine to Alta California immediately. This was impossible, Verger irritatingly maintained. They needed rest, training and adjustment. The somewhat heated exchange of letters finally led to compromise. Thirty men would be sent to California, twenty for Palou in Baja and ten for Serra in Alta. The new year, 1771, was but twenty days old when the *San Antonio* sailed again from San Blas for Alta with the ten new missionaries aboard.

In the meantime, back in Monterey, Serra's mounting urge to go forward was halted. Like a prisoner, he waited. That Monterey was not a favorable location for a mission became more apparent each day. But he must wait; wait for permission from the Viceroy to move it to the logical and more suitable spot, Carmel, three miles away. He must wait for the Indians. Small groups of natives came to the Monterey compound. They were friendly and readily accepted the *padre's* gifts, but they showed no eagerness to work. The major villages were at Carmel. Under the circumstances, no regular mission routine was possible. It would have to wait.

One bright moment came, however, on the 26th of December 1770. A native couple brought their five year old son to the mission asking that he be baptized. This, Serra's first Alta California baptism, was a fine Christmas present and a hopeful portent for the new year.

One of the Baja Indian boys, who had been associating with the Carmel natives soon discovered that he could understand their language. It was a language of sounds and "grunts" without benefit of alphabet, but out of it Serra formed a basic vocabulary; the key that opened the door of understanding. Serra now could translate the liturgy and Christian doctrinal teaching into the native tongue of the Carmel Indians. The dialogue worked both ways. In turn, the natives were using Spanish words and expressions. Serra always opened to them the arms of friendship, accompanied by small gifts and the greeting, "Amar a Dios!" (Love God!). This soon became the mutually accepted salutation not only between Spaniard and native, but among the Indians themselves. It was a delightful surprise to Spaniards just arriving in the new land to hear from the natives the familiar "Amar a Dios!" or "Vaya con Dios!" "Go with God!" In the west, is frequently heard the more abbreviated form, "Adios!"

The long, lonely days passed into weeks and weeks and months grew into a challenge of patience and endurance as no ship came with news or supplies from the outside world. Vegetables from Serra's and Fages' gardens provided sustenance when staples gave out. Spring had called green shoots from the earth with promise of abundant crops, only to wither and die before harvest. The new-comers had much to learn about growing wheat, corn and beans in Alta California. The flat land near the sea proved to be salty and though flowers bloomed profusely in the area more sunshine was essential to the hardier crops.

Almost two years after she had sailed away, the white sails of the *San Antonio* rose over the horizon and the little ship dropped anchor once more in the harbor of Monterey.

Ten new missionaries disembarked and Serra was jubilant. The first mail in two years included letters from Galvez and Verger. Serra had permission to move the San Carlos mission to Carmel and the doors were opened for new missions.

Fages had mail too. Of first interest to him was his commission as captain. This promotion was in keeping with his position as commander of the military in Alta California. A letter from Galvez told the commander that there should be no delay now in founding the new missions. Missionaries and supplies were aboard and Rivera was on his way to San Diego with more men. The long postponed San Buenaventura should be founded immediately: one mission between that and San Diego. San Antonio and San Luis Obispo should be established in the north and explorations should be made with the idea of starting new missions in the San Francisco Bay area. Agricultural tools were in the hold of the ship, church goods and all the necessary supplies required for the new missions. Galvez had backed up his commands with men, implements, tools, seeds and livestock.

In accordance with his directions, Father Serra assigned each of the new missionaries to his post. Fathers Pieras and Sitjar, both from Majorca, were to go to San Antonio; Fathers Cruzado and Paterna to San Buenaventura; Fathers Cambon and Somera to San Gabriel; Fathers Juncosa and Cavaller to San Luis Obispo; Fathers Dumetz and Jayme, also Majorcans, were to replace Fathers Parron and Gomez, who were ill and had asked permission to return to Mexico. Fages countersigned the assignments, giving his official seal of approval, then the documents were sent to Verger and Galvez.

Serra wrote each of these gentlemen a personal letter, which accompanied the legal documents. To Verger, his words were humble but insistent. Still more priests were needed, and he stressed the necessity of dependable and accelerated supply lines between Mexico and California. The new land was producing, but so far, barely enough for survival. Staples, hard goods, manufactured products must come from Mexico. The ships were slow and sailings dangerously far apart.

Serra urged Galvez's continued support. He understood the problems of the missions, perhaps better than anyone else outside of California and Serra could speak to him in confidence. Of himself, he wrote, "Would that it will not be less than I promise myself and the more I fear doing less, the greater is my desire to accomplish more." [2]

As soon as her vital cargo was unloaded, the *San Antonio* weighed anchor and set sail for San Diego. Fages and the missionaries assigned to the southern missions were aboard. But before Fages left, Serra had prevailed upon a favorable mood and had obtained his permission to found Mission San Antonio, during his absence.

The sails disappeared over the horizon. The next morning, July 8th, 1771, right after saying the Mass, the Father President set out with Fathers Pieras and Sitjar, seven soldiers, nine cows, two heifers and a bull, six calves, a sow, and male pig, a hen and chickens and eight mules. On the back of the mules were packed flour, chocolate, plows, seeds, candles, vestments, chalices, bells, all the necessary items for the embryo settlement, then the procession started down the dusty trail.

The Spaniards had developed an exceptionally fine, sturdy, well-built breed of mule, whose hardiness was specifically adapted to the arduous task of conquering the far reaches of the new world. The Spanish mule, along with

2. Geiger, op. cit., Vol. I, p. 276.

his muleteer, the man who trained, drove, fed, cared for and doctored the braying, balking, kicking beasts, were the unsung heroes of Spanish America. Surmounting towering obstacles of endless desert waste, foreboding mountains, steep, rocky canyons and swollen rivers, they blazed limitless miles of trail, opening the vast unknown domain for conquistador, explorer and missionary. Independent, stubborn, honery, the mule could be equally patient, long-suffering and faithful. With a little verbal persuasion, he carried his heavy load, ill-shapen but, skillfully balanced and professionally strapped around his belly, resolutely ploding single file, roped loosely to the animal ahead, as was the entire string, all rhythmically swinging in the path of the lead horse. Pounding, clicking, scraping, sliding, his sure-footed hooves grasped the rough, slippery earth with unbelievable dexterity and security, day after day, year after year, as long as his willing body could endure.

Traveling southwest, through the Santa Lucia Mountains, the missionary party came to a pleasant, wooded valley, which they named *Canada de los Robles,* Valley of the Oaks. The warm, penetrating valley sunshine was a welcome reward after long months in the cooler coastal climate of Monterey. Serra selected a spot which, to all appearances seemed suitable for a mission. A lively stream ran through the green valley. High grass and vegetation indicated fertile soil.

The Cross was raised and the bells were rung in the branches of a great oak tree, in preparation for the founding of Alta California's third mission. This was a moment of triumph, of hope; a moment apart from the frustrations, confinements and limitations that had held Serra captive the last two years, a moment under warm July sun; a moment of uninhibited freedom.

The bells rang out, loud, clear, their metallic song un-
dulating, reverberating through the awesome, empty silence;
the silence of a primordial, virginal land. Serra's spirit, all
his freedom loving heritage, his natural energy, his apostolic
zeal, his vocational dedication to the love of Christ seemed
to soar into one penetrating, clarion call. Chiming with the
clear rhythm of the bells, his sonorous voice, like a canticle,
called out to all who might hear them, to all who would
come in the years following, "Come, you pagans, come,
come to the holy Church, come, come to receive the Faith
of Jesus Christ!"[3]

The dedication ceremony that July 14th, 1771 was much
as usual, with one difference. During the sermon, Serra had
noticed a single Indian standing on a hill some distance away,
watching the proceedings. After the ceremonies Serra came
toward the native, offered him gifts and showed in sign
language that the priests and Spaniards wanted to be friends.
The Indian left, stoically but later returned with others of
his tribe. They brought gifts for the strangers and Mission
San Antonio seemed to be off to a good start.

Serra stayed on at the new mission for two weeks, helping
with the work of building and acquainting the *padres* with
their new tasks. They must begin immediately to learn the
native language in the meantime, accept the little manner-
isms that would lead to friendship with a people whose life
was completely foreign to their own. They would accept
the ways of the native, not force theirs on him. They would
eat his food, work beside him, teaching rough, untrained
hands to mold, build and construct shelter. Then they would
sing with him, pray with him, live with him, not as strangers,

3. Geiger, **op. cit.**, Vol. I, p. 280.

but as one of his own. With keen awareness of the natives' needs, capabilities and shortcomings, the priests related to native customs, habits, and ideas, keeping some, gradually eliminating others but using the best, always with the hope of alleviating the filth, suffering and want due to ignorance, which made their lives so deplorable.

Though painfully slow and awkward at first, the Indians' muscles and body gradually adapted to tools and the skills of the white man. In time, he too, could wield an axe, spade, shovel, cut and carry logs and put them together to build a house; he could press adobe blocks and form them into a church. Motivated by the very excitement and satisfaction of performance and the rewards of better living, they soon became proficient along many lines. They learned to swing a lasso, apply a branding iron, cinch the girth of a reluctant mule and hitch him to a plow. They learned to till the soil, plant seed and reap a harvest. And all this time, the liturgy and teaching of Christian doctrine was opening dark, sluggish minds to the knowledge and hope of Christian truths.

When the San Antonio fathers were securely sheltered in their temporary buildings, Serra took off for Monterey, leaving most of the military to guard the new mission. In Monterey, he quickly assembled a group of workers and went to Carmel to start work on Mission San Carlos de Borromeo de Carmelo, which would be his home mission from that time on.

For six busy, lonely months he worked with the few soldiers and workmen on hand along with the natives, clearing and leveling ground, cutting, hauling and nailing timbers into place, and thatching roofs. Relieved of Fages' nagging and autocratic rule, the soldiers worked diligently and cheerfully. Soon the work was done. Buildings took definite form and so did the missionary spirit. At every opportunity Serra talked to the natives, encouraging their friendship and gradually built the foundation and nucleus of a productive missionary life. On the 24th of August, 1771, he blessed the Cross and sang the High Mass of dedication.

But in southern California things were not going so well. Fages and the missionaries assigned to founding the new missions there had disembarked from the *San Antonio* at San Diego. Rivera, too, had come up from Baja with the soldiers commissioned for the founding of the new missions. Fages now had fifty men under his command. Everything was as Galvez had planned. There was no reason to postpone the overdue San Buenaventura. The missionaries were eager to go. It had been arranged that they would meet Serra at the site for the dedication. The arrangement agreed upon before the *San Antonio* had left Monterey included that Fages would send a military escort to Monterey for the Father President's land trip to San Buenaventura. No escort was sent. Instead, Fages kept his entire military group at San Diego.

This first of the California mission string had not recovered from its inherent difficulties. Many natives had turned in trust and friendship to the padres; conversions were increasing; baptisms and marriages were regularly performed; the most reliable families and workers had moved into the compound; the regular routine of missionary life was progressing.

But hundreds of Indians were still living in their original villages some distance from the mission. These were the thieving, mischievous, rebellious Indians whom the first Spaniards had encountered. Native converts from the compound had made regular visits to the outposts in a feeble attempt to teach them Christianity. This arrangement had never been approved by Serra and was totally unproductive. In fact, the very sight of their brothers receiving gifts and food from the missionaries in reward for their work infuriated the outland Indians and further stimulated bad feelings.

In fact the mission Indians were far from enjoying prosperity. The land surrounding the mission was poor. The water supply was inconstant. Crops had not been abundant. They had been able to partly feed themselves and even to share some with their outlying brothers. But food and supplies had been stretched to the utmost when the invasion came.

Rivera and all his men, Fages, the new missionaries all descended on the poor little mission struggling for sustenance. Word was sent to Monterey and that unit shared their dwindling supply with San Diego.

The two San Diego priests, Father Gomez and Father Parron, (who had been with Serra in Loreto and the early days at San Diego) were ill and waiting to return to Mexico. Fathers Paterna and Cruzado, assigned to San Buenaventura, were welcomed by the San Diego priests. They had no choice, however, but to await Fages' signal to go ahead; a signal which did not come. Reluctantly, however, he did agree that Fathers Cambon and Somera might go ahead with plans for the establishment of San Gabriel. He would not go with them. The two priests, accordingly, hustled around, assembling supplies and finally on the 6th of August, 1771, the four muleteers packed their reliable beasts of burden and with a ten man military guard and corporal, the two *padres* mounted and rode off into the north.

Josef Muench

Mission San Antonio de Padua. Recent restoration has recovered the beauty and charm of this early Spanish-California mission in a valley of California. Founded in 1771, it is again under the direction of the founding Franciscans.

For nine days they plodded mile after silent mile along the dusty Portola trail, civilization's only connecting thread through a vast, untamed emptiness. Then, on a quiet afternoon, they relaxed military formation to rest in a pleasant valley and examine possible mission sites in the area.

Suddenly, shattering the silence, a screaming, yelping, painted mob of wild Indians, armed with bows and arrows rushed toward them. Sensing danger, the soldiers scrambled for their leather packets and guns. One of the priests, poised, standing straight and tall, calmly walked toward the fiery natives and unrolled before them a large, realistic picture of Our Lady of Sorrows. The savages, either believing it to be a real mother and child or some kind of magic, stopped before the painting and threw away their arms. The chiefs laid gifts of beads before the likeness and calling other natives from nearby villages, they made signs of reverence and indicated they had come in peace and friendship. The Spaniards graciously accepted this abrupt change of attitude and reciprocated with kindly gestures and gifts, as substantial proof that their intentions also were entirely peaceful. Then they moved on toward their destination.

There was no mistaking the San Miguel Valley, so clearly and minutely described as a suitable spot for a mission. In fact, Crespi's diary so specifically describes landmarks that even today, historians can retrace the steps of these early pioneers through a maze of freeways and city skyscrapers. With a backdrop of precipitous blue mountains on the east, it was indeed a rich, fertile valley, crossed by two rivers. Trees of many kinds and tall grass, now brown in the autumn sun, covered the plain which gradually sloped down to the water's edge. Wild berries and grapes roused visions of future fruit orchards and nut groves. The *padres'* wildest imagination, however, could not have perceived that this embryonic core of western civilization, this tranquil, silent valley would one day be surrounded by one of the greatest cities of the world.

Visitors from all parts of the world today are fascinated by the magnificent San Gabriel Mission, moved in 1775 to its present site. Later known as the "Queen of the Missions," [4] its venerable facade, famous campanile and wealth of artifacts are devoutly preserved by the Claretian Fathers, who maintain it as a parish church. San Gabriel, a thriving, residential city, still maintains a quiet charm, reminiscent of the past, despite its proximity to the rushing, surging, buzz of freeway traffic. Its mountains and its river preserve the original name the *padres* gave this early mission site.

On September 8, 1771, Fathers Combon and Somera erected the Cross and said the Mass of dedication. The next day building began, with unexpected assistance. The Indians came, mingled with the soldiers and eagerly offered to help with the work. No doubt the workmen considered the unsolicited apprentices more of a hindrance than a help, but the more patient *padres* accepted this further gesture of good will as a favorable portent and directed their untrained energy into useful channels. In record time the temporary church and the house for the priests were finished. The presidio and corral soon followed, all enclosed by the usual stockade.

Unfortunately, the beneficent beginning was soon blighted. The Indians came in droves, delighting the *padres,* but the military took a dim view of this inundation of a dirty, disorderly, uncontrollable mob. In fact, the corporal was terrified and his fear was the cause of the violence he feared.

4. This term has also been applied to Mission Santa Barbara. Both were most productive and beautiful architectural specimens. Santa Barbara was founded after Father Serra's time.

He gave orders that no more than five Indians should be admitted inside the compound at one time.

The senseless order in one sudden grip not only halted, but contradicted all the *padres* had come to accomplish. Furthermore, the Indians regarded it as a contemptuous insult. They had built the mission. It was theirs. They had shown goodwill toward the white man and he had flaunted them with dishonor. The *padres* pled with the corporal, but to no avail.

About this time Fages arrived from San Diego on an inspection trip. The *padres* presented their case and he assented. The natives, by all means must be allowed inside the stockade. Otherwise, how could they receive instruction and training? Fages' hearty agreement with the *padres*, however, was pure histrionics. As he left the compound, he whispered orders to the corporal not to allow a single Indian inside the stockade.

It was a typical Fages' double-cross; an arbitrary usurpation of military power; disrespect for the authority of the *padres* and a defiant contradiction of the missionary effort he was commissioned to promote. As a result, the *padres* bottled up in the compound were exiled from the natives and the natives outside were deprived of the missionary leadership they had encouraged and welcomed.

Whether purposely or by accident, Fages had placed in command of the San Gabriel military unit a man of weak and immoral character. Fages had never shown any particular objection to the fraternization of his men with the Indians. In fact, there were times when he seemed to encourage it, if straying to Indian huts meant fewer men to feed in camp. This had always been one of the serious sources of conflict between Fages and the missionaries. Regulations absolutely forbade immoral association of the military with native women. Such acts were to be judged and punished by the *padres*. But Fages allowed the priests no authority over the military and despite Serra's insistence on strict moral conduct, Fages was inclined to overlook the incidents or to deal indulgently with them.

At San Gabriel, the problem was climaxed when one of the soldiers molested the wife of the chief. All evidence pointed to the corporal, himself.

One afternoon the soldiers were going about their daily routine of rounding up the horses outside the stockade, when suddenly Indians appeared from everywhere. The little group of Spaniards, taken totally by surprise, ran for their leather jackets and guns, but before they could get organized the mob of angry, painted natives armed with bows and arrows and showing every indication of being in a fighting mood had surrounded them. The corporal without waiting for a sign of peace or parley, pulled a gun and aimed. A shot rang out and the chief fell to the ground, dead.

This was not enough. They cut the head from the corpse and hung it from a pole, using the excuse that the gory sight would frighten the natives into submission. Eight of the soldiers followed the Indians as they fled, disarmed them and returned to camp. The horrified *padres* demanded the head be immediately removed from the pole, but the repugnance of the heinous act lived on.

The next day, October 11th, the entire horizon was a circle of fire. All the villages of the area had united in a signal, but unbelievably a signal of peace. Unlike the barbarous tribes the Spaniards had encountered in the Sonora country, the California Indians were actually a peaceful people. Seemingly aware of division between the military and the missionaries, they were casting their reliance on the *padres'* denunciation of the soldiers' misbehavior and violence and offered to make peace.

Again in late October, Fages came by San Gabriel. With him this time, were Fathers Paterna and Cruzado with the military guard assigned for the founding of the long postponed mission San Buenaventura. The lurid details of San Gabriel's "Indian hostilities" were colorfully expounded.

This news Fages hailed as factual justification for his past behavior. With the superiority of one who knew it all the time he declared, "Now San Buenaventura cannot be founded, nor indeed, San Luis Obispo, because I need the soldiers to reinforce this mission as well as San Antonio."[5] He left six more men at San Gabriel, a total of eighteen men with nothing to do.

Actually the corporal in charge at San Gabriel had been the source of all the trouble. When Serra heard of the situation, he sent his own trusted Corporal Joseph Maria Gongora from Carmel to take charge. Immediately the scene changed. Repairs and improvements were made to buildings; the natives resumed their contact with the missionaries, learned the usual arts of cultivation and building. Everyone agreed that the San Gabriel natives were very different from all the other California groups. Left to go ahead in peace, despite the darkened beginnings, San Gabriel became one of the most successful and productive of the mission chain.

Fages continued on to Monterey, arriving in November, after an absence of almost five months. On his way home, as he had promised at San Gabriel, he left more men at San Antonio. But he placed a corporal over them who was

5. Geiger, op. cit., Vol. I, pp. 306-307.

of much the same stamp as the first one in San Gabriel. The men refused to work; just loafed around. This situation resulted in the *padres* having more mouths to feed and no one to do the work. The *padres* and Indians turned carpenter, livestock keeper, muleteer and soldier.

Fages proceeded on to Monterey with the rest of the men, cattle, mules and bad news. Admitedly, Fages had problems. The additional men Rivera had recruited from Baja for military service in Alta California were of extremely low calibre. Many had been prisoners. As soon as they arrived in San Diego, they began to desert, some retracing their steps to Baja, others running off to the Indian camps. Those who stayed refused to work or loafed on the job. To rely on so weak a fortification for the protection of new missions was, to say the least, discouraging.

Still Fages' management of the men was responsible for most of the resentment and distrust among military ranks. He would order severe and unjust punishment for minor military infractions, while overlooking or actually encouraging immoral conduct. This along with his natural stubbornness and resentment of Serra's authority created a depressing situation. The thin line of defense gradually weakened. Animosity among the natives grew. They rightfully demanded restitution for Spanish abuses of their women. But particularly repugnant to the *padres* was the deplorable reality that so called Christian Spaniards were flauntingly breaking the very laws, ideals and customs the *padres* had come to instill among the natives.

To the zealous and dynamic Serra, the trouble at San Gabriel was distressing enough, the news that Fages had halted the founding of San Gabriel was distressing enough, but the news that Fages had halted the founding of San

Buenaventura again and refused to go ahead with San Luis Obispo was tragic.

Waiting, frustration, defiance. Serra's cross far exceeded that of physical pain. Despite all hindrances, Carmel was making progress. Great numbers of converts were receiving baptism, but the regular mission schedule was hindered by lack of supplies, complications of distances, delay in communications, government interference, but mostly by Fages.

Ignoring Fages' declaration at San Gabriel, Serra requested him to supply the six soldiers necessary for founding San Luis Obispo. Again, even with thirty-six soldiers idle at Monterey, Fages refused. He made one concession, however. Serra had been pushing the exploration of San Francisco Bay with the idea of determining favorable locations for the two proposed missions in that area. On the 25th of March, 1772, Fages, accompanied by the usual military and Father Crespi, as diarist and chaplain, set out to explore the San Francisco Bay region. They scouted along the seemingly endless, irregular, shoreline of the great waterway for miles reaching the east bay side and as far north as the outlet of the San Joaquin and Sacramento Rivers at what is now Carquinez Straight. Amazed at its extent, they concluded that it was impossible for a land party to reach the north shore of the bay, and that further exploration should be done by ship.

While they were still reconnoitering the inlets and tributaries of the vast San Francisco Bay, word came of serious famine in San Gabriel. When the northern missions had shared their meager allotment of supplies with San Diego in July, they had been left dangerously short. In fact, every mission in Alta California was in dire need of food and supplies, but San Gabriel was faced with starvation and revolt.

Galvez had planned that nine shipments of supplies and goods would arrive in California between 1769 and 1771. Due to disasters at sea, scurvy and a shortage of ships, four had arrived. It had been a year now since the *San Antonio's* last voyage and the number of hungry mouths had multiplied.

Fages hastily returned to Monterey, organized a group of his best marksmen and started out for the "Canada de los Osos," "Valley of the Bears," proposed site of Mission San Luis Obispo. The expedition was successful. They shot about thirty bears, dried the meat and distributed it among the missions most in need. The hunt also paid an unexpected dividend. The wild bears had been the age-old enemy of the defenseless natives. By exterminating the dreaded beasts, the Spaniards had won the lasting friendship of the San Luis Obispo Indians.

Seeds, milk and bear jerky managed to sustain life, but privation lasted into the summer of 1772. In August of that year, word came that the *San Carlos* and *San Antonio* were both anchored in San Diego harbor. *San Antonio's* orders were to sail on to Monterey, but treacherous head winds in the Santa Barbara channel forced her back to the southern port. Captain Perez, no less daring in 1772 than he had been in 1769, captained a ship that was not too sturdy when new. Now her timbers shivered with age and strain and his best judgment was to turn back. Serra wrote Palou, "Now we have everything in San Diego and nothing here."[6] There was no choice, they must bring the supplies from San Diego by mule train — a long, slow, tedious, almost impossible task.

Due to Serra's persistence and persuasive powers, Fages

6. Tibesar, 1, p. 265.

finally yielded. San Luis Obispo could be founded and he reluctantly promised that San Buenaventura would eventually be established.

Accordingly, on the 24th of August, 1772, Serra, Fages, Father Caveller, who had been assigned to the San Luis mission, and a ten year old Indian boy, whom Serra had baptized, along with a group of soldiers and muleteers started south.

On the first day of September, 1772, Serra blessed the Cross and said the Mass for the founding of the fifth mission of the chain, San Luis Obispo. Then they hurried on, leaving Father Caveller there alone with eight soldiers and a drastically meager bundle of supplies. More were promised and Father Junocosa was to come later with a corporal of the guard and four additional men. The bear hunt had opened the door for a friendly reception and Father Caveller began the usual building and teaching; and another group of human beings were introduced to the ways and thoughts of western civilization.

Serra had never before seen the Santa Barbara Channel Indians. He had heard Crespi, Fages, Portola, Perez and others tell of the great numbers of tall, sturdy natives of exceptionally good physique, their intelligence, advanced beyond those of the other Alta California tribes. Now, he saw them and he perceived beyond all his former aspirations, the compelling need for missions among these fine people. Thousands lived in the twenty Chumash villages; friendly, well-built, imaginative, active human beings waiting, ready for the teaching and the uplifting leadership of the missionaries. Serra speculated that at least three missions were needed in the area. To see them was to love them with the boundless love of his apostolic heart and he longed now more

Mission San Gabriel, fourth of Serra's missions, was founded in 1771. Controlling half a million acres from the mountains to the sea, it was for some twenty years one of the most prosperous of the chain. This present structure was built in 1806 and is now used as a parish church.

than ever before to bring them the love and the Faith of Christ.

They pushed on to San Gabriel, the only mission Serra had not seen. Fathers Cambon and Somera seemed to have overcome the dismal events of their beginning and things were going well. This tribe was distinct from all the others, but they seemed cooperative, and eager to learn, work and they were becoming Christians. As his arms reached out to them with gifts, his prayers reached to heaven in their behalf. In the blood relationship of prayer and sacrifice, these were his own. He congratulated the priests and reported to his superiors that this was, "Without doubt the most excellent mission site so far discovered."[7]

But San Gabriel still seemed to be the victim of some sort of military imbroglio. Serra learned from the priests that Fages had given secret orders to remove the estimable Corporal Gongora and replace him with the previous disreputable corporal who had caused so much trouble in the beginning. He went directly to Fages, who denied all knowledge of the matter. A letter, however, in Serra's possession, established undeniable proof and Fages finally admitted guilt and promised to allow Gongora to remain at San Gabriel.

The missionary President's duties extended from the exalted heights of offering the Holy Sacrifice of the Mass to the detection of the devious schemes of degraded corporals. They left San Gabriel secure and peaceful for the moment and continued on to San Diego. They made a fast trip, considering the usual speed of a mule train. For one thing, the animals carried no burden, and for another as we have previously observed, Fages was really a man of action

7. **Ibid.,** p. 359.

with the ability to move forward, when it was in his interest to do so.

Memories undoubtedly crowded Serra's mind of those first tragic days in San Diego as he compared the fragile beginning with the thriving settlement of 1772, now a busy rendezvous for ships, men and priests. Serra talked a bit with Fathers Crespi and Dumetz, who were there temporarily before going on to Monterey, and with the two mission priests, Fathers Jayme and Tomas de la Pena. But Serra had work to do and he wanted to get to it.

He went directly to see Perez and to persuade him to sail the *San Antonio* on to Monterey. He emphasized the desperate and immediate need in Monterey and the other northern missions. Mule trains were slow, awkward, and were limited to carrying smaller cargo. Bulky articles needed for agriculture and the churches must be transported by other means. Perez's knowledge of the northern seas and the fact that winter was coming on had convinced him it was not wise. Yet, Serra's personality, his zeal, and his irrefutable arguments finally moved Perez to agree to the northern trip. The *San Antonio* not only reached Monterey safely, but returned to San Blas without mishap. Another crisis had passed and the northern missions were saved.

Serra's next undertaking was to persuade Fages to agree to the founding of San Buenaventura. Here he was not so successful. Fages not only refused to consider the project, but he held both outgoing and incoming mail containing orders and information of the utmost importance.

This was the *coup de grace*. Fages had stiffled, restricted, and strangled the missionary development. All the missionaries agreed that the enterprise was doomed with Fages in

California. They urged Serra to go to Mexico and state his case before the Viceroy.

De Croix was no longer Viceroy, but Bucareli, his replacement, who had just arrived from Spain, was a zealous, sincere man of responsibility. He had heard there were strained relations between the military and religious in California and he was deeply concerned about the California project. Galvez had returned to Madrid because of illness. However, he still held an important post high in government circles and followed fervently and enthusiastically all news of the missions he had so expeditiously begun.

It was the psychological moment for Serra to go to Mexico. The missions had reached dead-end. Portola's warning to Fages to remember that the primary purpose of the Alta California conquest was to extend the faith had not only been ignored, it had been rejected. Now, the project lay paralyzed. Its revival and continuance depended on the success or failure of Serra's interview with the Viceroy in Mexico.

CHAPTER VIII
ALWAYS GO FORWARD

SERRA'S TRIP to San Diego, his insistence that Perez sail on to Monterey and the subsequent arrival of the *San Antonio* had saved the northern missions. Monterey had survived the crisis of 1772, but survival was not enough. The mission system, still in its infancy, must grow, move forward or die. Serra knew that Fages' autocratic control, his refusal to move ahead at this crucial time threatened the entire system. The outcome of his trip to Mexico would decide the fate of the Alta California Missions. In fact, his very determination to go had immediate effects.

Not until Serra boarded the *San Carlos* and sailed out of San Diego Bay on October 29, 1772, did Fages realize, to his horror, the weakness of his own position. He, the commander, now stood powerless before the humble, limping

Franciscan. The gray-frocked "visionary" had suddenly become a political entity, a power in the echelons of government. As the white sails faded over the horizon, Fages knew he was but a figure-head, disgraced, chastized, bereft of command.

He became a changed man. No longer filling the role of commander, his disguise as a blustering, military leader vanished. He appeared more generous, more tolerant, more sympathetic toward the *padres* and his own men.

The *San Carlos* made a fast trip to San Blas, arriving November 4th. Between San Blas and Mexico City, however, Serra must make a long, painstaking overland journey through miles of sparsely populated areas, flat barren lands, steaming jungles and steep, narrow mountain roads. Franciscan monasteries at intervals along the way provided pleasant and friendly hospitality. His first stop was in Tepic. Here Serra heard great news. The Dominican Order was taking over all Baja California missions. Father Palou and his Franciscans were free for service elsewhere. Serra wrote Palou, hoping soon they would be together in California. This was more than a hope. Due to communication gaps, Serra could not know that Verger had appointed Palou and six of his fellow missionaries to Alta and at the moment Serra was writing his letter, they were on route to Monterey.

Juan Bautista, a bright, young Indian boy, loyal and helpful to Serra, was making the trip with him. It was a great adventure for the boy, but somewhere along the way, no doubt in the mosquito infested jungle, both Juan and Serra contracted fever.

When they arrived at the monastery in Guadalupe, the two travelers were desperately ill. Certain.that death was imminent, the friars administered the last sacraments. As the burning fever tortuously enervated his sixty year old body, Serra thought and prayed for Juan. He was concerned, not only about the boy's welfare, for he had become very fond of him, but he was fearful of the effects at home, should the boy die. Understanding the Indian mind, he knew that in the minds of the parents and indeed the entire tribe, no possible explanation could ever remove the belief that the Spaniards had deliberately captured and planned to kill the boy. It could mean an entire Indian colony's rejection of everything Christian.

The boy recovered, no doubt due to Serra's prayers, dissolving that problem. Serra's fever subsided and despite the pleas and warnings of the friars, he was determined to continue his journey. Serra had never spared himself and he had work to do. He must go forward; never turn back.

It was an arduous trip, even for a younger, stronger man. When Serra reached Queretaro, the fever again raged and the relapse became extremely serious. There seemed no doubt now that his death was but a matter of hours or days. Serra prepared to meet his God, but prayed that he might finish this last task and return to Monterey. Eventually, the fever left his enfeebled body. He was spared, but the illness delayed his journey several months. But he was able to travel again. On February 6, 1773, he and Juan arrived at the College of San Fernando in Mexico City.

After the long, grueling journey, Serra, weak and wan, found security and solace in the well ordered monastic life of liturgical routine and discipline. The intellectual and cultural atmosphere of this center of spirituality was like coming home to a world far removed from the rugged frontier life of California. Indeed, San Fernando had been his New World home for a large part of the last twenty-four years. It was his destination when he left Palma for the New World. Again, San Fernando had been his headquarters after he left Sierra Gorda, and during the several years he had spent in Mexico preaching and teaching. He found friends there and memories. Father Verger, fellow Majorcan and confrere, welcomed the President of the California Missions with the reverence, respect and prestige due his present position, still remembering his former eminence and renown as Palman professor and Lullulian University orator. They reminisced over the difficulties of a Majorcan's gaining recognition in the foreign missionary field in 1749. Now, twenty-four years later, Verger was Guardian of the leading Franciscan missionary College in New Spain, Serra, Palou and Crespi held important posts in California and Majorcan Franciscans made up a large percentage of the entire New World missionary personnel.

Juan's eyes opened wide, as he looked, listened and observed strange sights and sounds of a world he never could have imagined. He was amazed by the great buildings and rushing crowds of the city, but he was especially surprised to see Spanish women. No white women had come to California. Now he knew these Spaniards had mothers, wives and sisters just as his own people. They were not born of mules, as his fathers had concluded. Juan found enough familiar sights and sounds in the strange land to feel a comfortable belonging. Their churches, though more majestic, had bells that rang much as did those of the missions and gray robed friars spoke in the same quiet, friendly manner. And as he had done at home, he spent the days helping Serra and praying, working and singing with the friars.

Serra's appetite and physical energy were slow to return. But his determination to pursue the object of his trip had not diminished. The friars pled with him to rest a few months, to wait until his strength returned, until he was refreshed in mind and body. But Serra held tenaciously to the accomplishment of his mission. To Verger, he reported in detail the events, activities, results, the plight and the California dilemma. He outlined his program of changes and adjustments, his hopes and his plans. Verger, whose letters may have sounded stolidly pragmatic and unimaginative, was zealously devoted to the missionary ideal. He under-stood Serra's problems, approved the entire program and urged Serra to see Bucareli as soon as possible. The rugged years of frontier life had not diminished Serra's polished diplomatic acumen, his charm, and ready wit. Nor had they dulled those brilliant persuasive powers, for which he was noted in Palma, in Mexico City and in California. His conferences with Antonio Maria Bucareli Ursua, gentleman from the courts of Madrid and newly appointed Viceroy of New Spain, took place in the splendor of the Royal Palace of Mexico City in March.

A devout Christian, Bucareli was totally sympathetic with the missionary project of California. Judging from the disturbing rumors he had heard and the confusing official letters he had received from Fages, he had concluded much should be set right and was eager to know what were the true facts. Serra's direct and impartial truthfulness matched his zeal, his enthusiasm and his practical knowledge of affairs. The viceroy was impressed by his effectual suggestions and wise judgment. He gave the *padre* sufficient time to state his case. The conferences were not only congenial, but fruitful, both for the government and for the missions.

Their first consideration was California's life-line. Men, animals and missions require food and other necessities. Since no over-land routes had been established, the sea lanes to Monterey and San Diego were of vital importance and the number of ships and sailings must be increased to keep the struggling missions alive through these critical initial years.

Bucareli had been advised that the port of San Blas was badly situated, its needed improvements would be too costly; it had never been and never would be a suitable harbor. Upon this advice he had all but decided to abandon it. Serra attempted to convince the Viceory that without San Blas, California would become an orphan, with no communication, no source of supply. Serra's first victory was Bucareli's agreement to maintain San Blas, at least for the present.

Granted that San Blas was not an ideal harbor and that sea lanes alone could not support the growing needs of the new colony, Serra accentuated the importance of opening land routes to California. This was not a new idea. Galvez had launched the California project on this premise. Spanish soldiers had died in Sonora Indian wars that this might be accomplished. It had been the topic of conversation and conferences in government and military circles for years. But no definite action had been taken.

Serra reminded the Viceroy that Indian relations were particularly favorable at this time and that Colonel Don Juan Bautista de Anza, commander of the presidio at Tubac, would be a most able leader for such a project. He stressed the importance of government financing and the issuance of

Josef Muench

Though some have been restored several times, all of Father Serra's missions still stand. San Luis Obisbo, now laced by pepper trees, shows little of the hardships of its early beginnings.

authoritative orders for the establishment of an overland route from Sonora to Monterey.

The Viceroy assured Serra of his cooperation in these and all other subjects discussed and asked that Serra put his ideas and demands in writing. This Serra gladly did.

Back in the seclusion of San Fernando he worked resolutely, spelling out point by point in thirty-two well defined legal terms the specific rights of the Indians, the duties and responsibilities of the soldiers, their privileges, and restrictions, including punishment to be administered for transgression. He recommended that one hundred men be sent to California immediately; that their pay be increased and that special inducements be given married men who wished to become permanent residents.

He defined the duties, restrictions and qualifications of military men, post office officials, missionaries, colonists, even stating the personal characteristics necessary for the governor of the frontier missionary project. Serra's *Representacion* had all the aspects of important legal documents prepared by Spain's best attorneys at law. The limping *padre* from California had demonstrated a new qualification not before observed.

Signed March 13, 1773, the *Representacion* became the "Constitution" of the missionary movement from that time on. All government officials and all missionaries were bound to abide by it. Bucareli's recommendation to the Viceregal Council that it be ratified in its entirety was accepted by that august body and later, it was signed and approved by the king.

This marked the coming of age of the California project. The missionary movement was no longer an experiment, a dream. It had acquired legal status; all points of procedure were specifically defined; it had won the respectful attention and regard of Spanish officials as a permanent and valuable entity of the Spanish Empire.

Everything had gone well. The trip to Mexico City had been a triumph, but Serra made one mistake. Both leaders had agreed that Fages must be removed from office. But Serra, in a moment of over-confidence and anxiety for smooth future operation in California, surrendered his diplomatic suavity and acumen by naming as his choice for the position, Sergeant Ortega.

The politically wise missionary president should have remembered that every high governmental official covets his inimitable and undeniable prerogative of naming appointees. Bucareli rejected Ortega. He explained that his inferior rank as sergeant disqualified him for so important a post. Then Bucareli proposed the name of Rivera. Ortega, supposed discoverer of San Francisco Bay and Portola's right hand man, no doubt would have been an able commander. Serra had known Rivera in Baja and on the expedition to Alta. He offered no objections to the man. But this brief slip of diplomacy would result in agonizing problems in the years to come.

Aside from this unfortunate selection, Serra had won the fundamental purpose of his journey, the vital point that "the government control and education of the baptized Indians should belong exclusively to the missionaries."[1]

Rooted in Christian doctrine and nourished by its charity, the missions could advance only under religious leadership. Without spiritual motivation they could degenerate into military fortresses or government slave camps. Serra felt to

1. Decree of Bucareli and Council, Mexico, May 6, 1773.

have obtained an irrefutable, legally formalized statement on this vital issue alone, merited his long, painful, hazardous trip.

Grateful for a successful outcome of his earnest pilgrimage, the still weak and pale, sixty-year-old *padre* and his eager Indian companion, Juan, prepared for their homeward journey. The San Fernando fathers attempted to persuade him to stay for a time. He needed rest and time to recuperate and they needed him. They wanted to elect him Guardian of San Fernando. Indicative of their regard for him, is the following letter, written by Father Pablo Font, of the College of San Fernando, in August 1773:

> The Father-President Junipero Serra is a religious of the Observant order, a man of very venerable age, formerly professor at the University of Palma, who during twenty-four years, since he has been a missionary of this college, has never spared himself in toiling for the conversion of the faithful and the unfaithful. Notwithstanding his many and laborious years, he has the qualities of a lion, which surrenders only to fever. Neither the habitual indispositions from which he suffers, especially in the chest and in difficulty of breathing, nor the wounds in his feet and legs have been able to detain him a moment from his apostolic tasks. He had astonished us during his recent sojourn, for, although very sick, he never failed, day or night, to take part in the choir, much less when he had fever. We have seen him apparently dead, only to be almost immediately revived. If now and then he attended to the needs of bodily health at the infirmary, it was only because he was ordered to go there. Sometimes, in his journeys among the faithful and the un-

faithful he has become so ill, on account of wounds and other infirmities, that it was necessary to carry him on a stretcher, but he did not wish to stop to cure his half dead body; and soon he would be restored to health, through the influence of Divine Providence alone.

In truth, on account of these things, and because of the austerity of his life, his humility, charity, and other virtues, he now is returning, as if it were nothing, to Monterey, a distance of a thousand leagues by sea and land, to visit those missions and rejoice them by his presence and by the measures which he had procured and to preside over them and found other missions until he shall die. May God grant him many years of life. Much more could I say of this holy man. He has at various times been elected Father Superior, but was never confirmed, either on account of his absence or because the prelates thought it wiser not to withdraw such an extraordinary man from his apostolic tasks.[2]

Appreciative of his brothers' concern and affection, but still more certain of his destiny, Serra could give no consideration to lingering in an atmosphere of esteem and ease. He wanted only to return to his people, to be of service to them, and to be among them as quickly as possible. The Indians of California needed him far more than did his Franciscan brothers in Mexico City.

Perez, former captain of the *San Antonio* and Serra's good friend, has been given command of a new frigate, the *Santiago,* which was scheduled to sail on her maiden voyage in January of the new year. The *padre* and Juan retraced

2. Chapman, **History of California, The Spanish Period,** p. 358.

their treacherous overland path back to San Blas, where they boarded the ship and safely arrived in San Diego in March, 1774.

Once again the sight of white sails on San Diego's horizon signified restoration of life for the Alta California Missions. Hunger, in varying degrees, had been their companion from the beginning. Crops had matured in the new land, but because of increased demands, the supply problem continued to be serious.

The *Santiago's* arrival not only meant a fresh and bountiful stock of food. It meant the coming of desperately needed people: a doctor, artisans, skilled tradesmen and the first white women and children to step on California soil. So, the coming of the *Santiago* marked the transition of status. California was no longer a frontier camp. It was now a Spanish settlement.

Deeply stirred to have safely returned to San Diego, Serra took time to evaluate conditions there and to discuss immediate problems with his good friends, fellow Majorcans, Father Jayme and Father Fuster, then he continued overland, on to Carmel, stopping at each mission along the way. He noted remarkable progress everywhere. The natives, who had no agricultural background in their thousands of years of existence, were now beginning to learn the delicate art of stirring the earth to produce food. In the warmth of the sun, seeds were sprouting and the earth, carpeted in its brilliant, new green, gave promise of another budding spring.

But the most welcome and impelling news to Serra, was that Anza, the renowned army officer, Spanish cavalier and tough Indian fighter, had arrived in California! In fact, the sandled, gray-robed Franciscan leader met the bronzed, hardy frontiersman just outside San Gabriel. The stocky, be-medalled Captain, fighter, victor and peacemaker among the most savage Indian tribes, with characteristic courtly Spanish grace and chivalry, doffed his great plumed hat to the *padre.* As the two leaders stopped by the dusty California trail for a brief exchange of greetings, each was deeply aware of the implications of this historic moment. These two courageous trail blazers had many characteristics in common. Through their magnanimous self-sacrifice, their dynamic enterprise, initiative, zeal and enduring patience it had been possible to extend European Christian civilization to the far western shores of a new continent.

Anza's presence there was due in part to the Indian boy, Sebastian Tarabel, a Baja Indian, who had run away from San Gabriel, crossed the Colorado desert and made his way to Anza's headquarters at Tubac, near Tuscon. If this boy could make his way from west to east, Anza reasoned, surely, with the help and guidance of Father Garces, friend and devotee of the Yumas, they could make their way from east to west. To those who were fully aware, as were these two leaders of the tense, bloody history of the wild desert country through which the Anza party had come, this opening of a land route into California was one of the great triumphs in the winning of the west.

Soon after the first Spanish ships and conquistadors arrived in New Spain, Jesuit and Franciscan missionaries and explorers penetrated the land of the Upper Pimas, the Apaches and the Comanches. They built missions, churches and schools. Tremendous progress both spiritual and material was made among the wild savages of the territory now known as Sonora in Mexico and Texas, New Mexico and Arizona in the United States. This comparative peaceful operation lasted approximately two hundred years.

Then in 1751, a veritable hell broke out. The English and French were pressing in from the east and north. Wars, colonial competition and long built up national hatreds contributed to the violence known as the Indian Wars. Jealous politicans, ambitious fur traders and trappers incited the tribes into rebellion against the Spanish. Spanish colonists disrespectful of Indian land and rights, aggravated the burning fuse. Comanches, supplied with guns, attacked Apaches. Hatred and passions rose into unspeakable violence and horrendous atrocities. Attacked by one tribe, then another, all Spanish people, including priests, colonists, and soldiers were massacred. The savages mutilated the bodies and ate human flesh. Missions, churches, schools, homes and villages were burned and plundered.

Punitive military support was slow in coming. Procrastination, lethargy and disorganization among political officials delayed action and often, when the action finally came, it further antagonized the natives and seemingly justified the accusations of their enemies. Sonora and the entire region became a wild desert of horror, closed to all except the military.

Anza's grandfather, an officer in the military, had served in Sonora. His father was killed by Apaches there. Anza knew the land, the Indians and the geography of the place. He had long dreamed of opening a route to California.

In 1770-71 Father Garces, a zealous and dynamic Franciscan missionary priest, explored the territory of the Colorado and made friends of the Yumas, a tribe of gigantic, fierce, warlike people with long, coarse, black hair. The Yumas controlled the mouth of the Colorado river and had so far prevented whites from crossing into California. But Palma, their chief, coveted the missionaries' gifts and believed there were advantages to having a mission. Father Garces promised Palma that a mission would follow providing he would allow the Spaniards to cross the Colorado at that point. In the meantime, Hugh O'Conor, whom Galvez had sent into Sonora to subdue the Apaches had met with some success.

Anza had spoken to Bucareli, pleading the case of the land route to California before Serra made the trip to Mexico. The timing was right. Serra's subsequent insistence that the California settlements could not survive on supplies sent by ship alone, had come at the precise moment when the stage was set. Bucareli kept his promise to Serra, government funds and orders sent Anza on his way. Anza's party, consisting of thirty-four persons, including Fathers Garces and Diaz, arrived at San Gabriel March 22, 1774. Now that the overland route was established, Bucareli urged immediate colonization. Government aid would supply each colonist with livestock, a salary equal to the military and land of his own. Two missions would be founded in the vicinity of San Francisco and pueblos or towns would be established.

Palou was at Monterey when Serra came home on the 11th of May. As the two good friends embraced, each remembered Serra's farewell at Baja, "Until we meet in Monterey."[3] The *Santiago,* like a homing pigeon was riding at anchor in Monterey Bay, and the warehouses were filled with supplies from her hold.

Palou and six of the Baja Franciscans had arrived seven months before. Verger had suggested Palou take charge of the missions until Serra's return. Fages had mellowed and worked with Palou to keep things working smoothly, as Serra observed on his trip home from San Diego.

3. Geiger, **op. cit.**, Vol. I, p. 62.

The results of Serra's mission to Mexico City followed closely behind him. Twelve days after his homecoming, he was to greet Fernando Rivera y Moncada. California was no stranger to Rivera, nor was he a stranger to Californians. He was the same Rivera who had led the second land expedition to California in 1769 and who, again, had brought men and livestock up from Baja in 1771. Serra had first met the lieutenant as commander in charge of mission property under Portola in Baja during the interim between the Jesuit exit and the Franciscan arrival. This relationship had little to recommend him.

Neither was Rivera pleased over his California assignment. He had hoped to retire, because he was not well, and had settled down in a chosen Baja location, where he bought a new home. All his money was invested in this venture. His family had no desire to move to the raw frontier and Rivera's financial condition was negative. He was forced to borrow the money for transportation. Nonetheless, a military man obeys orders and when Bucareli requested that he go to California, he promptly complied. Fages quietly rode off to San Diego, where he sailed on the *San Antonio* to San Blas.

Spain's urge for exploration was not yet dead. Authorities in Madrid, still worried about the encroachment of the Russians along the northern shore, had ordered Perez to sail the *Santiago* as far north as the sixtieth parallel, to examine the coast for possible foreign invasion, to chart the so far unchartered seas and to make observations of the native life in that part of the new territory.

The seasoned master mariner, well aware of the hazards of such a voyage, made of Serra a sentimental request. Would he say Mass under the famous Monterey Oak, first sanctified by Viscaino's three Carmelite Fathers in 1602, then again by Serra, June 3, 1770, in the first Monterey Mass of the California expedition. It was an hour of memories, especially for Conisarez, Crespi, Serra and Perez, and the others who had attended Serra's first Mass there four years before, almost to the day.

Although adverse winds and rough seas forced Perez back at the fifty-fifth parallel, he had planted the Spanish flag on the island, now known as Canada's Queen Charlotte; he had chartered the entire coast line; he had made a complete and favorable report of the Indian tribes along the coast, whom he described as friendly, well built people, and he had seen no Russians. To have established the assurance that California so far was not threatened by foreign powers, was heartening news to Monterey, Mexico City and Madrid. Perez and the *Santiago* safely arrived back in San Blas in November.

These northern explorations in defense of the last, far western Spanish colony were but flickering shadows of the vigorous push that had built an insignificant coalition of provinces into the greatest empire in the world. Spain's penetration into the western hemisphere had come two hundred years before colonialism impelled other European powers into expansion. Now those powers were vigorously aggressive and Spain, tired and impoverished, was facing dark days. Still, she showed periodic flashes of her old vivacity.

By 1774, another darkness was taking over, the darkness of materialism. Spiritual ideals were becoming subordinate to the lust of wealth and power. Spain needed money, but most of all, she needed men — men who had not forgotten the idealism and the driving force of the old days.

Men like Serra and Galvez had dreamed a dream, a

dream often claimed outwardly by others, spoken in words but not in deeds. Bucareli had been sincere with Serra, but Bucareli was a political appointee and looked to the future advancement of Bucareli. Rivera, too, who had claimed admiration for the missionary movement, actually was never in favor of any part of it. Concerned with his own comfort and ease, Rivera resented his appointment to California. He had flatly refused to consider the founding of new missions. Despite Serra's persuasion and direct orders from Bucareli that he should proceed immediately with the long delayed San Buenaventura and the new San Francisco missions, nothing was done.

"What are we doing here, since it is plain that with this man in charge, no new mission will ever be established?"[4] lamented Serra. His hands were tied. Furthermore, Rivera refused to carry out the rules of the *Representacion,* or to cooperate with the missionary fathers. Still since the day that Portola sailed out of Monterey Bay, the missions had been beset with obstinate, recalcitrant military commanders; men who regarded the Indian as a troublesome, dirty, worthless savage, and who had little sympathy with the idea of christianizing them.

In the face of all handicaps, there was no denying the progress and the growth of the missions. They had rooted. No one man could stop their development. He might thwart it. He might bind the branches and prune the main limbs, but the missions were solidly established in California. By this time, a mutually intuitive understanding between native and *padre* had evolved into a corporate determination and tenacity that would ultimately lead to their maturity.

4. Tibesar, **Serra's Letter to Father Guardian,** Vol. II, p. 111.

Josef Muench

Reflected in the fountain are several of the old mission bells at the
Mission San Juan Capistrano. Still in use they peal, with their lovely
old voices, ringing out today's hours and reminding us of yesterday's.

Men who had known hunger and the necessity of subsisting on whatever was available, were producing food for themselves and enjoying the felicity of a full stomach and well-stocked larder. There was an abundance of milk and the women were learning to feed their children nourishing food and to keep them clean.

Serra was particularly concerned with the children. He wrote Bucareli, "The spectacle of seeing about a hundred young children of about the same age praying and answering individually all the questions asked on Christian doctrine, hearing them sing, seeing them going about clothed in cotton and woolen garments, playing happily and who deal with the *padres* so intimately as if they had always known them, is indeed, something moving, a thing for which God is to be thanked."[5]

Serra longed to push it all ahead faster and farther. But if progress had been slow, he could take comfort from the knowledge that neither he nor the missions were turning back. And portents and signs indicated that Spanish enterprise was not yet dead.

---

5. Tibesar, **Serra's Letter to Bucareli,** August 24, 1774, Vol. II, p. 139.

CHAPTER IX
CALIFORNIA COMES OF AGE

*T*HE IMPACT OF Serra's conversations with Bucareli had penetrated far beyond the walls of Mexico City's Royal Palace. The pale, ailing *padre,* his eyes burning with earnest resolution, had convinced Bucareli of California's illimitable hopes.

Born of a sense of history and the vision of leadership Serra's intelligent appraisals and his practical suggestions impressed Bucareli as both basically realistic and vitally important. Consequently, the Viceroy informed Madrid that once rival European powers discovered the vast potential of this western empire, nationalistic aspirations would lead to aggression and belligerence.

And sharpening the focus on Bucareli's admonitions, Madrid had word of Anza's successful crossing from Sonora to California and various glowing reports concerning the versatility, extent and unique beauty of San Francisco Bay.

Carlos III's orders to Galvez to investigate possibilities for the occupation of California issued from fear of Russian invasion. Now, six years later it was obvious to all officialdom that the Empire's problems had multiplied and Madrid sent repeated warnings to Bucareli to secure the coast of California.

Perez had assured the absence of foreign settlements as far north as the fifty-fifth parallel. But under the circumstances, Bucareli was not satisfied. Suddenly the heretofore remote California missions became a valuable political entity and Spanish explorers again ventured on unknown seas.

This new flicker of Spain's olden days was purely defensive, an operation of sleuthing rather than aggression; of fear rather than conquest. Still attributed to it was the essence of adventure and its hazards and hardships were comparable to those of the fifteenth century.

Based upon Serra's evaluation of San Blas as a necessary base of operations, Spain's best naval officers were sent to transform the swampy, crumbling harbor into a safe, efficient and permanent port.

By the first of the new year, ships began to sail from the reconditioned naval base. The *San Antonio* once again sailed into San Diego Bay loaded with welcome supplies. The *San Carlos* followed in June. She stopped at Monterey but only long enough to unload supplies and mail. Bucareli had sent separate documents to Rivera and Serra containing specific instructions to establish two missions and a presidio in the San Francisco area without delay. Captain Juan Bautista de Ayala's orders were to sail the *San Carlos* into San Francisco Bay and to explore, survey and chart the entire area.

Rough seas and a rocky coastline had kept previous mariners well out to sea. Also the narrow channel, with hills rising abruptly in the east gave the impression from the sea that there was no opening there. In 1595, the Philippine explorer, Captain Cermeno of the *San Augustine* reached the small bay to the north of Point Reyes. Here the chaplain, Father Concepcion, had said Mass and they named the bay Puerto de San Francisco. The party remained in the harbor a month, making repairs and building a small boat for reconnoitering. On November 30, a violent storm wrecked the *San Augustine* and most of the crew were lost. Cermeno and the few survivors sailed south on the newly completed *San Buenaventura* which had escaped serious damage.

In this same harbor Sir Francis Drake later anchored to repair his ship. The bay is now known as Drake's Bay.[1]

Ayala, approaching the narrow channel, now known as the Golden Gate, with extreme caution, lowered a small boat for reconnoitering. The boat was quickly swept into the bay by the incoming tide and the *San Carlos* followed, the first ship to enter the great harbor.

The handsomely carved and decorated Spanish ship, riding high in the smooth water, its sails fluttering in a gentle breeze, seemed dwarfed by the magnitude of the inland sea. Even more impressive from the surface than from the hill tops above, calm, quiet, surrounded by low hills, it extended as far as they could see. Crespi had not exaggerated when he had said it would hold all the ships of Spain. Certainly it was a potential center of world trade and a providential spot for a great city.

Choosing a large island, now known as Angel Island

1. There is no authentic proof that Drake entered San Francisco Bay.

as headquarters, they spent forty days reconnoitering, exploring, charting and mapping coves, inlets, small bays and the great river (Sacramento-San Joaquin) that pours into the harbor.

Plans had called for a rendezvous with the Anza-Rivera land party but they saw no signs of them. Neither had they heard of Rivera's involvements which prevented the meeting. They found the flag, Cross and note left by Rivera and Father Palou on their exploratory trip the year before. Deciding something prevented the planned 1775 trip, Ayala and the *San Carlos* returned to Monterey.

In the meantime, Bucareli had sent another exploration party into north seas. The *Santiago* and *Sonora*, sailing from San Blas in March 1775, had orders not to stop at San Diego or Monterey, but to proceed together as far north as possible. They kept as close to the shoreline as possible, investigating bays and coves for signs of foreign settlements. Some of the roughest seas are off the shores of California and in July the two ships became separated. The *Santiago* reached the forty-ninth parallel before sickness among the crew forced her to turn back. She had made one important discovery, however, a great river emptying into the Pacific from the east. Could this (the Columbia River) be the hoped for water passage from east to west across the continent?

The more successful *Sonora* reached the fifty-eighth parallel and had discovered a fine harbor now known as Klokachef Sound in Alaska. Neither had found any sign of foreign visitors or settlers. Each headed for Monterey on its return and the two ships were reunited there in August. The *Sonora* had reached the extreme northern boundary of Spain's encroachment, her final exploratory effort. The

Betty Berg Favello

Mission Dolores in San Francisco. The old mission stands at the left and a newer church, bearing the same name stands at the right. Worn stone floors of the interior of the old mission bear the marks of many years of bare-footed worshippers.

flag and the Cross planted there were left for others to find, nor did Spain pursue those northern discoveries.

But in a sense, Spanish interests did move north. The focus now was not on Baja California, not on San Diego, not on Monterey. The focus was on San Francisco Bay. Ecela, one of the officers of the *Santiago,* was sufficiently interested in seeing the famed harbor from land to organize a party, including Father Palou. Following the route traveled by Rivera and Palou the year before, they explored the shoreline and surrounding country. Rivera's adamant decision that it was not a suitable location for a mission or pueblo did not agree with their findings, nor, indeed with those of any of the other groups that visited the area. The Ecela party just missed the *San Carlos* but found the papers left by the officers and concluded, rightly, that they had returned to Monterey.

Three Spanish ships lay at anchor in Monterey Bay at one time. This was an unprecedented event for the isolated group of Caucasians at Monterey. Implicit to a ship is an aura of romance and these three had special significance. First of all, they bore testimony that no foreign power threatened their settlements; the ships, their officers and men were links with the world from which this group had long been separated; and they directly represented the Viceroy, commander, arbiter, ruler, and sole support; furthermore, they had come in the name of the King of Spain.

It called for celebrations! Everyone was in fiesta mood. Rivera banqueted the explorers with all the pomp, etiquette, splendor and courtly grace this far outpost would allow. Serra invited them to Carmel where he spread his best table and generously entertained them with his typical affability, wit and charm. Fat beeves and lambs were slaughtered. Vegetables, fruit and berries were brought in from the gardens, fish fresh from the sea and wine, the best wines of Spain. Spirits were high and the men of the sea had tales to tell of their adventures and of the people they had seen along the northern coasts.

Serra was their most attentive listener. The natives, large of stature, well built, sturdy, agile, bearded were fairly intelligent and friendly. The Mission President sang the Mass of thanksgiving and transcendentally adopted those newly discovered people of the north. The same immutable urge that had sent him from Palma half-a-world across the sea, that same intonation from within flared anew, not dimmed but nourished by age, hardship, discouragement and distance. He spoke of planting missions all along the northern coast. Those tall, friendly people were ready to learn trades, to build, to use their dormant minds and to teach their fingers and hands new skills, new means of producing food and of living. They were waiting to learn of the living Christ, of God's love and of eternity. Why should not this project go forward? It was Spain's best assurance of safe and secure Pacific shores. But no one heard!

The days of festivity were soon over. One by one each ship set white sails against blue skies and drifted out of view. The quiet of abandoned hopes settled down on the striving community and the monotonous pattern of life resumed its rhythmical routine. Summer mellowed into fall.

Just before sailing time, Juan Perez, navigator of the *Santiago,* became seriously ill. Shipmates and landsmen pled with him to remain in Monterey but the seasoned mariner was determined to sail with his ship. Two days out of Monterey he died. A fellow Majorcan, one of Serra's best friends and one of California's most resolute and conscientious heroes was gone, buried at sea, where he had spent most of his life. Time after time, the missionary project had hinged on the daring, proficiency and sagacity of this noble master mariner. Along with Portola, Crespi, Palou, Galvez and Serra, Captain Juan Perez should be remembered by historians as indispensable to the Spanish era in California.

Even as the ships were drifting out of the California scene, a landsman was making history. Anza, the renowned Indian fighter, peacemaker and trail blazer was proving equally adept as an organizer and leader of colonists.

Anza moved while Palma's promise of safe passage still held. He assembled two-hundred-forty colonists of varying background: some Indian, some African, the rest Spanish or of mixed Spanish and Indian blood, now making up much of the population of the frontier. With them, supplied at government expense, went one thousand animals, horses, mules, sheep, pigs and cattle, along with supplies, clothing, tools, building materials and tools for farming. The men, expected to serve as a supplemental military force, when needed, received military pay.

They left Tubas October 23, 1775. The first night out a baby boy was born. When they arrived at San Gabriel, sixteen hundred miles of desert, mountains and untold hardships later, they were two-hundred-forty-four strong. Eight children were born enroute; one mother died in childbirth and three others perished.

Anza chose this time to travel down the Santa Cruz River to the Gila and to follow the Gila to the junction with the Colorado. This route assured fresh water all the way but pasture was short, resulting in some loss of livestock.

When they reached the Colorado, the river was at flood and crossing seemed impossible. Scouting the area, Anza found that, further up stream, the river divided into three branches, one of which was sufficiently shallow for the entire party to cross without mishap.

Palma came out to greet his friends and was rewarded with a fine gift from Bucareli, himself. It was a sleeveless cloak of blue cloth, lined with gold, a jacket and trousers of chamois skin, two shirts and a cap with the same coat of arms worn by the Spanish dragoons. The situation was a bit touchy. Palma was gracious and most grateful for his gift, but he insisted that his people have missions and his attitude was adamant and ominous.

Father Garces' intentions of founding missions among the Yumas had always been sincere. But government promises of supplies and soldiers never seemed to materialize. Father Garces and Father Eixarch staked their lives on the untenable guarantee that missions would be established and remained at the Yuma camp.

Anza's party probably faced the most difficult part of their journey after crossing the river. High mountains, white with snow, loomed ahead. The weather turned bitterly cold and it rained. Anza scouted for the best paths, helped the weaker members of the party over the critical passages, encouraged and assured them that all would be well. And most important, as other excursions have learned, he kept them all together. The long, steep climb was successfully completed and the descent into California was easier. The weather was warmer and the grass greener. On January 4, 1775, they reached San Gabriel.

The bells rang; all the bells clamored the glad news, loud and long. The first colonists had successfully made the overland crossing into California. Everyone turned out, priest, Indians, soldiers came to welcome the newcomers and to celebrate the great occasion. Everyone, that is, except Rivera.

Rivera had new problems, which left him more irascible than ever. On top of everything, Anza's coming at this time would force the issue of establishing missions in the San Francisco area. Rivera had repeatedly opposed extending the mission system beyond Monterey. Again on his return from San Francisco, the year before, he had stated emphatically the area was not suitable for missions. Despite these decisions, Serra had urged him to found a mission there. Then provoking his aggravation further was Bucareli's letter, demanding that the San Francisco missions be founded immediately. Anza's coming did not set well with Rivera.

While the ships were still in Monterey Bay and the Anza party was struggling across barren deserts, Serra had again pressed the issue of founding new missions. Four of Palou's Baja California priests still awaited assignments. Rivera's argument that he had too few military was justified on the grounds that Bucareli had not sent the one hundred men he had promised. To off-set this, Serra proposed that six of his guard at San Carlos could be spared and that San Diego could spare six more. With these men, they could found one mission at San Buenaventura. Rivera refused, but finally yielded to the *padre's* tenacious persuasion by a compromise. He would agree to founding one mission at San Juan Capistrano, half way between San Gabriel and San Diego.

Serra's persistence, aside from religious zeal, was pure logic. Time was running out: his years were numbered; the Spanish government was showing every sign of weakness and lack of funds; and colonists were coming. In other localities he had seen that the entire mission system had broken down, due to a few troublesome colonists. Now the Indians were in the mood for missions. If he could complete the California mission ladder without these long interruptions, the Indians, trained in a variety of skills, could soon cope with the inevitable influx of colonists. Rivera, on the other hand, was responsible for keeping peace among increasing numbers of unpredictable, wild savages with an extremely limited and scattered militia. There was, too, the unwritten and unspoken matter of authority. Rivera, supposedly top man, actually had authority only over a handful of soldiers. The bulk of the population, the Indians, under the mission system, were subject to the *padres*. The real collision course was one of power. The governor, regardless of name, resented the power of the *padres* and limited it as much as possible without falling into disrepute with the Viceroy. Serra, not concerned with authority wanted only to keep peace and progress with the work of conversion.

In accordance with Rivera's concession to found San Juan Capistrano, Father Lasuen (who had served under Serra in Baja and one of the six who had come with Palou), along with Sergeant Ortega from San Diego and twelve soldiers, arrived at the location selected for the mission on October 29, 1775. They raised the Cross, blessed it and said the Mass of dedication. The natives showed every sign of friendliness and even offered to help with the work. In a short time, the corral for the livestock was completed and the foundations laid for the buildings. San Juan Capistrano seemed to be to a fine start. Then word came of terror at San Diego.

Ortega and his men were to return at once. This meant Capistrano must be abandoned, at least for the time. They buried the bells and other non-perishable supplies and rushed back to the scene of trouble.

A dissident, runaway mission Indian, named San Carlos, (a name obviously repeated for ships, missions and men) led the uprising. The aboriginal agitator poured his grievances out in fighting, explosive words, fused with hatred and venom. The Spaniards would soon control all the tribes, he told them. They must kill, burn and run them out. His fiery words found sympathetic ears among the outlying villages, still restive, resentful, malicious and jealous of the better living conditions of the valley mission Indians. San Carlos, triumphant in his new feeling of leadership, proposed and organized a massive attack against the pitfully vulnerable mission.

There was a chill in the air, that night of November 5, 1775. The moon was bright. About eight hundred wild, painted Indians, armed with bows and arrows, slithered down the slopes into the encampment on the flat land. They formed two groups. The first was to attack the guard house and presidio. The other would seize the mission about five miles away.

The first group surrounded the guardhouse, knocked out a guard and set a signal fire, then their bravado evaporated. The rest of the guards were asleep; so were all the soldiers inside the building, but for some reason the natives fled.

The other group descended on the mission about 1:30 A.M. while everyone there was asleep, they looted the warehouse and sacristy, taking supplies, heavily embroidered vestments, chalices and all the valuable goods, acquired with such pain. This they gave the women to carry back to the villages, while the men fired the buildings. Constructed of logs, with thatched roofs, they quickly exploded into flame. The two priests, a carpenter and four soldiers, the only ones on hand, went into action. Using any solid barricade they could find, they fired into the mass of savages, spewing arrows all around. The carpenter was killed and two soldiers wounded but the seven men drove off the hundreds of Indians. Father Fuster, who fought beside the soldiers, as burning beams were falling all around, wrote later, "That night seemed as long as the pains of purgatory."

Father Jayme, believing his presence would calm the savages, went out into the open, calling to them, "Amar a Dios, hijos," ("Love God, my children"). These were his last words. The Indians seized him, stripped off all clothing but his underwear, shot numerous arrows into his body, then brutally pounded his face to pulp with rocks and clubs. Father Luis Jayme, a Majorcan, was the first missionary martyr of California.

No doubt San Carlos deliberately staged the rebellion during Ortega's absence. Without him, military discipline was relaxed and the presidio guard holds the historical distinction of sleeping through the entire melee. Routine communication between the mission and the presidio by means of bells and bugle calls were a daily occurrence. But on this particular night nothing, not fire nor murder nor gun shot nor savage shrieks had disturbed the military.

News of the disaster did not reach Rivera, at Monterey until December 15, a month and eight days afterward. Rivera immediately took the message to Serra at Carmel, personally. Rivera was fiercely angry and demanded reprisals equal to the violence of the crime. Serra, on the other hand, realized that severe punishment would only lead to more violence. It was useless to reason with Rivera in his present trauma, but Serra prepared to go to San Diego. Father Fuster needed his advice and consolation and Serra could prevent drastic reprisals. Rivera, knowing this, refused a military escort for the missionary president.

Rivera's party happened to reach San Gabriel the day before Anza's arrival from Tubac. This explains Rivera's attitude upon seeing Anza. Anza, the old Indian fighter, came to Rivera's assistance. Showing force at a time like this was important. Anza, with seventeen of his men and Father Font accompanied Rivera and his ten men to the troubled mission.

By February, he felt he had served the cause of San Diego and returned to his colonists at San Gabriel. Actually, the Spaniards feared the Indian tribes of the back country, perhaps thousands, might be involved in this thing. The show of military strength may have discouraged them. However, it seems more probable that it was limited to those who had heard the fiery voice of San Carlos. At any rate, there was no further trouble.

Anza and his group proceeded northward, receiving an enthusiastic welcome at each mission with, "the festive peal of the good bells." [2]

After stopping at Carmel, they went on to San Francisco. Father Font wrote his impressions, "The port of San Francisco is a marvel of nature and might well be called the harbor of harbors." And from a vantage point above the Golden Gate, he observes, "Indeed, although in all my travels I saw very good sites and beautiful country, I saw none which pleased me as much as this. And I think that if it could be well settled like Europe, there would not be anything more beautiful ... and the harbor so remarkable and so spa-

2. All quotes on this page from Father Font's Diary, **Bolton-Anza's California Expedition,** pp. 392-5.

Betty Berg Favello

Entrance to the new Mission Dolores, San Francisco, noted for its beautiful Spanish Baroque style.

cious that in it may be established shipyards, docks and anything that may be wished." [3]

The point from which Font made his observations was
chosen for the presidio, the vicinity of the present United
States Army Presidio of San Francisco. Further down the
peninsula, they came to "a beautiful arroyo which because
it was Friday of Sorrows, we called the Arroyo de los Dolores." [4]

Later, Mission Dolores was established there. The original mission was on what is now Eighteenth Street in the
"Mission District." A stream ran through there at the time.
The present Mission Dolores, built later, is on Sixteenth
Street and Dolores. The graves, the smooth stone floor worn
by bare-footed or sandled worshipers still speaks of the days
of the *padres* who were dedicating their lives to bring some
light to the lives of the natives.

The sites were chosen. Anza's force of men was far more
impressive than any of Rivera's individual mission groups.
Still, although they selected the sites for both presidio and
mission, they did not found them without Rivera's consent.
They returned to Carmel early in April, at the time Rivera's
reprisals were reaching a climax in San Diego.

San Carlos, after months of long, cumbersome trials, admitted it was he who led the revolt. But he sought sanctuary
in the temporary church. The *padres* had no desire to defend
the culprit, but church sanctuary, by tradition and by canon
law was a sacred thing. This, they would defend with their
lives.

Rivera was determined. In defiance of church law and

3. **Ibid.**
4. **Ibid.**

admonitions of the *padres,* he, with a military guard, forced
his way into the church and seized the offender. By this
action, he brought automatic excommunication upon himself
and all his military personnel who had taken part in the
episode.

Nine months after the disaster, Serra took passage on
the *San Antonio* and arrived in San Diego. At the sight
of the Father President, Rivera suffered a seizure of shudder-
ing dread. The sudden realization of his guilt overwhelmed
him. He had disobeyed every rule of *Representacion;* he had
defied Bucareli's orders; he had thwarted the mission project
which he had been assigned to assist and defend; and he
had succeeded in getting himself excommunicated. This however, by this time, had been resolved. Would Serra go to
Mexico City, as he had in the case of Fages?

But this was not necessary. Rumors of Rivera's conduct
had reached Bucareli and the government officials in the
Capital City. Agitated though he was, he added one more
black mark to his record.

A neutral observer, Captain Diego de Chaquet, of the
San Antonio, could see that San Diego needed new buildings
more than reprisals and offered the help of his twenty sailors
for the time they were in port. As long as Rivera would
furnish the armed guard, they would work with the priests and
Indians in the reconstruction of the mission. With the extra
hands, they made seven thousand adobe bricks, excavated,
leveled and laid foundations for the new buildings, in only
eighteen days. A few more days of this organized plan of
work would have completed the job. But Rivera heard rumors of Indian uprisings, or used this as an excuse. He ordered the military guard back to the presidio and refused to
supply another. No uprising materialized and the *San An-*

tonio sailed away leaving the work to the unconscionably slow process of native labor.

Military reinforcements came from Loreto and Rivera had no alternative but to rebuild San Diego, reestablish San Juan Capistrano and establish the San Francisco missions.

On November 1, 1776, Serra sang the High Mass of dedication and California's seventh mission at San Juan Capistrano was reestablished. The sixth, at San Francisco, had been founded in the interim. Anza and his colonists had been more than patient. Finally, Anza returned to Sonora and left Moraga in charge of the colonists, with orders to proceed with the foundation of the mission, presidio and colony. The presidio was established in June. On October 9, 1776, three months after the colonies on the east coast had signed the Declaration of Independence, Mission Dolores de San Francisco was founded. Actually, everything but the official establishment had been done in June.

Rivera received another letter from Bucareli about this time, stating that he presumed both missions and the presidio at San Francisco had been founded. This threw another fit of fear into the commander and as he traveled from San Diego he was relieved and gratified to know the mission and presidio had been founded.

Santa Clara, the eighth mission of the chain was founded on the 12th of January, 1777 and the pueblo of San Jose, nearby, was settled by Anza's colonists.

By 1777, eight years after her beginning, Alta California had surpassed Baja in growth and stature. Eight missions were growing and prospering and California had become an institution. Nothing could stop her progress now.

Three years earlier, in 1774, Galvez had sugggested that

Altar in Mission Dolores. The old carved wooden altar which was brought from Mexico in 1780, only 4 years after the founding of the Mission San Francisco De Asis (commonly called Dolores) is still beautiful and the painting on the ceiling is still the original.

Monterey should become the Capital of both the Californias and that the Governor should reside there. That same year, Bucareli appointed Felipe de Neve as Governor of California. Since Galvez's suggestion had not yet become official, Neve resided in Loreto, but was instructed to maintain friendly relations with the commander and the priests of both provinces.

In August of 1775, orders from the King made Monterey the official capital of the province and Neve was informed that he should reside there, but he did not receive the orders until December of 1776. He arrived in February 1777 with orders to: abolish prescribed punishment for the Indians involved in the San Diego uprising; to found the missions of San Francisco and Santa Clara; see to the founding of Santa Barbara Channel missions; encourage foundations of pueblos, or towns; advance agriculture in the missions and in the pueblos; consult Bucareli with regard to Serra's suggestions and needs. The new governor's first official act was to visit the President of the California missions, Father Junipero Serra at Carmel.

"A new optimism runs through his letters during the ensuing months that recalls the ebulient spirit of those first ones written from Monterey peninsula in 1770,"[5] writes Father Geiger. Rivera's resignation was automatic and he was appointed Lieutenant Governor, with residence at Loreto.

California's coming of age seemed too great a problem for Madrid. In an effort to identify with the development of the west; a royal decree established a new Viceroyalty, including California with Sinaloa, Sonora, Texas and New

5. Geiger, **op. cit.**, Vol. II, p. 147.

Mexico. This might have been a satisfactory arrangement had they appointed a man of vision and understanding as Viceroy.

As it turned out, California lost the cooperation and friendship of Bucareli and was now under the jurisdiction of Teodoro de Croix, nephew of Carlos de Croix of the early days. The nephew was not the same calibre as his uncle. However, Neve had the judgment to follow Bucareli's instruction and ignored the impractical and damaging suggestions of the new Viceroy.

Antonio Bucareli died in April 1779. His wise counsel, Christian principles, understanding and practical guidance had served the California project for fourteen years. His coastal vigilance and protective explorations not only contributed to the safety and progress of Spanish California but helped to preserve that territory for later possession of the United States of America.

CHAPTER X
THE BELLS TOLL

*C*ONFIRMATION, ONE OF THE seven sacraments of the Catholic Church, is usually administered by a bishop. However, on occasions, where a bishop was not available, the privilege has been extended to missionary priests in foreign lands.

When Serra was assigned to Baja California in 1768 he learned that the privilege had been given the President of the Jesuit missions there. Accordingly, he petitioned, through his Franciscan College of San Fernando, for the same privilege. Rome granted the permission in 1774 but all appointments of the Church were subject to approval of the Spanish government. The papers, consequently, requiring signatures from the king to the Guardian of San Fernando, gathered dust on official desks while Christian Indians were passing on to the next world without benefit of the sacrament.

Four years after Rome's approval, the *Santiago,* which anchored in San Francisco Bay, brought the official document empowering Serra to administer the sacrament for a period of ten years. Only six of the ten years were left. It had long been Serra's hope to bestow on every baptized California Christian the grace of the Holy Spirit through this sacrament. Now, that he had the power, he was determined to lose no time. It had never occurred to the Missionary President to regard this new privilege as a personal honor, comparable to a higher degree or a title of distinction. He simply regarded it as an instrument of grace for his converts.

In the simple language they understood, he had related to the natives the meaning and purpose of Baptism. Perhaps they failed to comprehend the theology, but due to the ineffable harmony between the sacraments and human nature, the basic truths found recognition; that living in faithless darkness, they could become children of God; that in their world of need and problems, baptism gave them assurance of the protective guidance of a loving Father — God; that as men, they had the capability of rising from savage to a civilized state; that by virtue of their humanity, they were qualified to love their neighbor and love their God. The signs, the formalities, the water, the salt, the symbols as well as the words of the sacrament witnessed to the ultimate truth of the Incarnation that Christ was indeed alive and present among them, waiting to be recognized. Through the teaching, the prayers, the songs, they gradually absorbed the understanding, the recognition of the love of God for them and felt, in return, their love and supplication going out to him in trust and faith.

Christianization is lifting the natural, animal-like human being to the knowledge of Christ. It opens to him the knowledge that above and beyond his actual grubbing for food and shelter, each person is a free and responsible individual with special dignity and the right to fulfill his talents and to live in the hope of an eternal home and destiny.

As baptized members of the communal mission life, with the church as its center, they had made progress. Now, Serra hoped, through the sacrament of confirmation, they would receive further strength, the spiritual strength of the Holy Spirit, a grace needed individually and collectively for the adult maturity of their Christian faith. He would leave them with the sacramental grace for their coming of age.

We have followed the Majorcan from infancy through an exemplary life of faith and courage: the simplicity of his inspirationally religious home life; the total giving of himself to the love of God in his calling to the priesthood; the perseverance and consummate dedication through his training years; the brilliant success of his teaching, which resulted in unsought fame and renown; the zealous fulfillment of that love and selfless dedication in his missionary career. We have felt with him hope and disappointment; joy and sorrow; frustration and suffering and we have seen that he endured each cross with Christlike patience, humility and peace. Father Serra's acceptance of the gray robe of St. Francis was no immature formality, no following of a pattern of style or custom, no pretense or intelligentsia, or sophistication. His was a true priestly vocation.

In his administration of the sacrament of confirmation, Father Serra reveals, as never before, his true self: in his consecration to prayer, his constant self-sacrifice, never compromising with human comforts, his simplicity and above all, the sincerity of his love of Christ and of those he had come to serve. He deeply and totally loved souls and he seemed to feel an obligation to render to each of the souls in his care the sacrament. It was, in a way, his last will and testament to them; his gift of grace from God, through him to them, to strengthen and sustain them with divine guidance and mercy.

In this spirit he began his tour, first to San Carlos, his home mission. The word filtered through the mission; the bells rang assembly and all the families came to the church. The priests heard confessions, then, assisted by Fathers Crespi and Dumetz, Serra sang the High Mass with solemnity and dignity. The congregation joined in the singing and prayers and the *padre* spoke to them, simply explaining profound truths partly in Spanish and partly in their own tongue.

In August, he sailed on the *Santiago* to San Diego, where he spent twelve days confirming, repeating the ceremony of San Carlos. Then, by land, he "climbed the ladder" of missions, San Juan Capistrano, San Gabriel, through the still untamed populous Santa Barbara area to San Luis Obispo, San Antonio, arriving home just two days before Christmas. Since June, he had confirmed one-thousand-eight-hundred-ninety-seven souls.

By 1779, San Francisco had become the favored harbor, leaving Monterey more or less deserted. In fact, as Serra planned his confirmation tour to the bay area, two ships lay at anchor there. One of Bucareli's last acts was to send two more exploration vessels out of San Blas for northern waters. They had both sailed together, reaching Alaska and returning to San Francisco in September. Both captains and chaplains were anxious to see the famous Father Serra and waited in port for his coming.

The old leg infection became so acute Serra at first sent word he must postpone the trip, then his determination over-

Mission San Juan Capistrano, Southern California. The only mission church used by Father Serra still standing, this chapel was built in 1777. An early Spanish altar, richly carved and covered with pale gold foil lends a soft radiance.

came agony and he arrived in Santa Clara October 11. Four days later he reached Mission Dolores. On each occasion, after singing the High Mass and preaching a fervent sermon, he confirmed all baptized adults who had not received the sacrament. Thirty-nine seamen received confirmation that day besides the forty-nine soldiers and one hundred and one Indians and their families.

During the long ceremonies, Serra seemed oblivious to the pain, but when the doctors examined it they said it was a miracle that he could even stand on so terribly an inflamed leg. He would not submit to treatment, for which we do not blame him. Eighteenth century medical science was far from a panacea for pain or infection.

Word came, while Serra was in San Francisco, that Spain, again at war with England, was, through her alliance with France, helping the American colonies fight for freedom. To the Majorcan *padre,* whose long tradition had been one of independence, this seemed a noble cause, but perhaps at this time, one his country could ill afford.

Serra had his own problems of freedom. Governor Neve, a man who insisted on technicalities and "fine print interpretations" had questioned Serra's papers authorizing his right to confirm. He did not question Serra's legal right, but he insisted on seeing the original documents with the required signatures. Mail efficiency had not improved, neither had official filing systems. To locate the original papers and to deliver them into Neve's hands would no doubt take the remainder of Serra's term of authorization. So the arguments persisted and Serra proceeded to confirm. However, at this time Neve's insistence was becoming a serious issue. Serra returned by way of Santa Clara, confirming all who had not received the sacrament on the previous stop, then waited at Carmel for permission from Neve to continue.

In all aspects of the Spanish government were ominous indications that the cherished past was gone. The temper of the age was secularism, lack of direction and purpose and individual advancement.

A tragic example of stupidity and shortsightedness among government officials occurred at Yuma. Bucareli was dead; Anza had been transferred to the Rio Grande and de Croix seemed totally incapable of coping with the responsibilities of his office. Father Garces and his companion, who volunteered to stay with the Yumas, teaching and interceding with the government in behalf of the Yumas' request for missions, had been abandoned. Year after year Garces pled, reasoned, begged and emphasized the importance of establishing missions and presidios among the Yumas.

This was a warlike tribe. Only the friendship of Palma had kept the peace. They grew more restless each year and Palma was losing face among his people. Only military aid, supplies, including gifts for the natives would maintain peace.

Vacillating, confused, careless and indifferent, de Croix produced only promises. That communication lines between Sonora and California were vital, did not seem to concern him. When he did order missions to be built, he specified that they be situated on the California side of the river. He gave no orders for a presidio, leaving them defenseless and at the same time irritating the Yumas who demanded missions on their side of the river.

The entire setup invited trouble. The Sonora Indian Wars had established the fact that sheltering colonists with their wives and children in the same compound with the Indian neophytes would not work. The colonists would "borrow" the Indian horses, then demand that the Indians be punished for retrieving their own stock. Aggravation, discontent led to further trouble.

De Croix had ordered Rivera to recruit additional settlers and militia for Yuma. Their arrival in June only multiplied the problem. The settlers, who regarded the Indians as use-less, dirty, lazy barbarians, ignored native claims to land and livestock, intensifying an inflammable solution.

On July 17, 1781, the fuse blew off. The naturally blood-thirsty Yumas defied all restraint. Armed, painted for war, screaming and whooping, they swooped on the compound. They killed every Spanish soldier and male settler, took all the women and children prisoners. They killed Rivera, then threw his horribly beaten and mutilated body into the river. They set fire to the readily combustible mission buildings and brutally murdered Fathers Diaz and Moreno.

The next day they were back again. They burned the remaining building and with war clubs, beat Father Garces and Father Barraneche to death. It is said that Palma held the mutilated body of Father Garces in his arms and wept. This could well be true. Father Garces, explorer, trail blazer and missionary priest had befriended Palma and his Yumas. He had staked his life as guarantee that his government would send protection and build missions among them. His heroic self-abnegation ranks closely to that of the Jesuit trail blazer and martyr of the southwest, Father Kino.

The Yuma massacre forever closed the land route be-tween Sonora and California. Fortunately, by this time, Calif-ornia had become self-sustaining. Plans made at the con-ference in Mexico City between Serra and Bucareli for

Anza's march to San Gabriel had given the missions their crucial boost and sustaining push. Mails would be agonizingly slow; scarcity of hardware, utensils and other manufactured items would curtail building and the physical progress of isolated communities. But through the missions Christian civilization and European culture had sunk deep roots on the west coast of the American continent. The Yuma insurrection would not stop their growth. However, it did halt all possibility of a vigorous Spanish forward movement and it prevented establishment of a strong European military arm on the Pacific coast. California would progress as a peaceful Christian settlement, awaiting the eventual advent of the Americans.

Ultimately, Neve's scruples regarding Serra's right to confirm were resolved. On August 16, 1781, Serra received letters from both de Croix and Neve reestablishing his permission to administer the sacrament.

As he had done before, Serra started at home base, then he was on the road again. First he visited the northern missions, San Antonio, Santa Clara and San Francisco. For Father Crespi, who accompanied him, this was in a sense, a sentimental journey. It was his first sight of San Francisco since his discovery expedition with Portola in 1769 and he was delighted to see his old schoolmate and life-long friend Father Palou again. For Father Crespi, the trip was one of those mysterious gifts that eludes definition, a bit of prediction about it, for in a few days after their return to Carmel, Crespi became seriously ill and on January 1, 1782, he died. Crespi, who had been in Alta since the first expedition in 1769, will be known in history as the diarist of the Spanish conquest of the west. He had participated in and left detailed accounts of all the major explorations. Besides the Portola expeditions, he had traveled with Fages through the San Joaquin Valley and was the diarist on the first sea exploration of Alaska. Altogether, his travels covered more miles than Coronado's and his narration of the scenes, topography, people and experiences are invaluable to history. From the time he entered the monastery of San Francisco in Palma, Serra had been his model. Many of the years he spent in the New World, teaching, baptizing, training had been beside or near his former instructor and model. Serra buried his beloved friend, pupil and fellow missionary in the sanctuary of the church of San Carlos at Carmel, where it is today.

One of Neve's orders, when he took office, was to establish communities of settlers, pueblos or towns. Idealistically, colonists from Mexico, supported for a time by the government, would engage in farming and produce food for themselves and the military. Consequently, on September 4, 1781, Neve founded the village of Los Angeles. Named for the Blessed Virgin, it was called Nuestra Senora de los Angeles, Our Lady of the Angels. Not far from San Gabriel, it was the beginning of the great metropolis of the west.

Unfortunately, many of the first settlers did not succeed in their devised function. In fact, the missions supplied food for themselves, the military and the colonists. Not trained or qualified for the rigors of frontier life nor provided with competent leaders, most of the colonists eventually returned to Mexico. Some, however, survived and established roots for others to come. The site was well chosen, as is confirmed by the busy, roaring city of today.

Serra was touring the southern missions, confirming, advising and encouraging his fellow missionaries, when Neve received orders from de Croix to found three missions in the long neglected Santa Barbara area. The Chumas and

Canalino Indians had been of special interest to Serra since the beginning. He had never ceased to plead for missions for these people, of higher mentality and ability than the natives of other sections. Bucareli too had continued his insistence in communications to de Croix, stressing the importance and necessity of establishing missions there. On Easter Sunday, March 31, 1782, it was Serra's great joy to bless the site, raise the cross and say the Mass of dedication for San Buenaventura, the ninth mission and Serra's last. No governor could refuse to found a mission ordered by the Viceroy, but he could delay its founding. San Buenaventura, the third mission Galvez had ordered to be founded in 1769, was truly delayed by the succession of governors. Serra's hope of thirteen years had at last been realized.

Santa Barbara was established a month later, "This new mission and Royal Presidio of Santa Barbara." Actually, Santa Barbara was a presidio only. Neve was in fact opposed to the mission system and would not set a date for the founding of the Santa Barbara mission. This was, of course, a dire disappointment to Serra. Furthermore, La Purissimo, the third mission ordered by de Croix in the Santa Barbara Channel was but a future dream.

Neve's influence was far reaching. In May, 1782, Serra received a most disturbing letter from the Guardian of San Fernando, which outlined Neve's future plans for the missions. There would be but one priest to each establishment; he would only visit the Indians in their hovels, speak to those who wanted to hear and retire. No instructions in agriculture, trades or religion would be held at the missions, and no new missions were to be established. Serra knew this would end the mission system.

But the little world of the western seaboard was changing

in the years 1782-83. De Croix was appointed Viceroy of Peru, Neve was made commandant general of the Provinces Internas and went to Sonora; Fages was named Governor of California. Fages, now a wiser and more cooperative man, wanted to work with the friars but before he left, Neve gave Fages secret orders: he must maintain peace among the natives (implying stiff punishment commensurate to the infraction); he should develop the Santa Barbara Channel by establishing more civilian pueblos; soldiers must not fraternize with the priests. This was a far cry from Portola's farewell advice. Fortunately, Spanish officials seemed to take orders lightly, interpreting them to their own convenience and judgment.

Before his right to confirm would expire, July 10, 1784, Serra was determined to make one more round of the missions. His bronchitis had become acute. His friends advised against such a long, arduous journey. But his anxiety to bring the grace of the sacrament to his "children" superseded regard for his health. In June 1783, he boarded the ship *La Favorita* and sailed to San Diego. After having administered the sacrament there he went to San Gabriel, where he became seriously ill. Still he continued to say Mass, baptize and confirm.

Then he went on to the new mission of San Buenaventura, a source of great joy and satisfaction, then to the presidio at Santa Barbara, San Luis Obispo, San Antonio and home. He remained at San Carlos four months before going on to Santa Clara and San Francisco. Returning by way of Santa Clara again, he dedicated a new church with Governor Fages representing the government. All of this would have tasked the energy of a younger, hardier man. Since receiving permission to confirm in June 1778, he had administered the

Betty Berg Favello

Altar at the Mission San Carlos. Father Junipero Serra, Father Juan Crespi and Father Francisco de Lasuen are buried here.

sacrament to five thousand-two-hundred-seventy-five.

At Santa Clara, Serra felt that death was near. He rested a few days then asked Palou to stay with him. He made his confession, spent the days in spiritual exercises and returned to San Carlos.

Father Serra had made his last journey. He could look upon the accomplishments of the last fifteen years with gratitude. Despite disappointments, harassments, delays and dissent, Alta California now had nine missions, four presidios and two pueblos. Cattle in abundance roamed the fertile lands. The missions not only supplied their own but had a surplus. Prosperity had supplanted poverty and starvation.

In a land where the name of Jesus had not yet been heard, there was now a climate of Christianity. Each day began and closed with the ringing of the bells, calling men to prayer. Mass was the first activity of the day, the Mass in which, according to Catholic faith, the living Christ, redeemer of mankind was present on the altar and remained present in the sanctuary in the Blessed Sacrament.

The Christian message as related to the natives, had given them the knowledge that each was an individual, a unique personality, a person loved by God. He learned that God heard his individual prayers for guidance and protection and that life was more than the search for fish and acorns. And he learned by the example of the *padres* that peace was better than killing, stealing and the disruption of the social order.

"Amar a Dios," "Vaya con Dios," 'Bienvenidos Amigos," the watchword of the new civilization, centered attention on his peoples' love of God, their dependence and trust in Him — and their love for each other in a Christian sense. The missionary project was far short of Serra's dreams, hopes and goals, so pitifully incommensurate with his vision of what might have been. Still he held no bitterness, only gratitude.

Serra sent for Father Palou. When Palou arrived August 18, the *padre* was not only suffering severe discomfort from the bronchial pneumonia, but the leg infection was extremely inflamed and swollen. Still he prayed and followed his spiritual exercises as though he were in good health. Palou chanced to remark to one of the soldiers, "It does not seem that the Father President is very sick." The soldier replied, "Father, there is no basis for hope. He is ill. The saintly priest is always well when it comes to praying and singing but he is nearly finished."[1]

For two weeks the two Majorcan friends talked of many things. Serra kept the conversation on mission problems: Neve's recommendations, the shortage of priests from Spain, the new diocese of Sonora, with jurisdiction over California, the delays of founding new missions. In a way, he was briefing his successor. Though these problems were vexing, Serra had faced greater ones. His trust in the providence of Almighty God and his calm, inner peace transmitted to Palou the fortitude he needed now and would need in the days to come.

The *San Carlos* had just anchored at Monterey. The ship's doctor immediately came to examine the Missionary President. As was the medical practice of the day, he cauterized his chest, adding to the pain and still not diminishing his illness.

One afternoon an old Indian woman asked to see the *padre*. Serra patiently listened to her woes, which seemed

1. Palou, op. cit., p. 266.

mostly that she was cold, then he gave her a blanket. Later it was learned that he had torn his only blanket in two and had given half to the eighty year old Indian woman.

For over a week the Father President suffered extreme difficulty in breathing. Still he gave no outward signs or complaints. As usual, he arose at dawn on the morning of August 27, reciting his breviary. He asked Palou to give him Viaticum, the last sacrament of the church. But rather than having Palou bring it to him, he insisted on going to the church. Wearing a white stole over his gray habit, he walked to the church, entered the sanctuary and knelt on a prie-dieu prepared for him. He sang the *Tantum Ergo* with full, firm voice, received general absolution and the Sacred Host. After some time in prayer, he returned to his room.

Sleep was impossible that night because of the intense pain. He knelt beside his narrow plank bed, with his chest pressed against the rough boards, and spent the long hours in prayer and meditation.

The next morning he had company. The officers of the *San Carlos,* his good friends of many years, came to pay their respects. First, he asked that the bells ring in their honor, then he arose and greeted the men in his usual cordial, gracious manner, giving no sign that he was seriously ill.

About noon he asked Palou to read the deathbed prayers. For a time he had been shaken by a great fear, then he told Palou, "Thanks be to God, thanks be to God, all fear has left me. I have no fear. Let us go outside."[2] At siesta, he lay down on the rough boards that were his bed, covered himself with the half blanket and placed the Crucifix on

2. **Ibid.**, p. 271.

his breast. After lunch Palou looked in to see if his friend needed anything. "I found him as we left him a little before, but now asleep in the Lord."[3]

That afternoon the bells of San Carlos Mission tolled the solemn, mournful, monotones of death. Quickly, the news spread. Father Junipero Serra, President of the California Missions was dead. Spaniards, Indians, half-breeds, soldiers, sailors, everyone who could come to pay respects to "Santo Padre, Bendito Padre," the "Saintly Father, the Good, Blessed Father."

Six hundred Indians attended the funeral the next morning. They came from Carmel, Monterey, San Antonio and the outlying villages to pray for the *padre* they loved. All those who had come the day before and many others paid tribute to the great missionary whose reputation now extended throughout most of New Spain. The ship's cannons fired "Salute" echoed by the bells' solemn tolling of "Doble," the mournful song of death. Father Palou sang the solemn Requiem Mass and delivered an affectionate, moving sermon. Then they buried the Majorcan, who had left his home half-a-world away to bring Christ's message of love and mercy to the heathen. His body was placed in the San Carlos sanctuary next to Father Crespi's.

For him was not the glorification of renown but the loneliness and hunger of a remote frontier; not the ease and comfort of an establishment but half-a-blanket on a straw mattress and plank bed; not a tiara and ermine trimmed robe but sandals and a cross.

Serra had lived in California only fifteen years but his work was the beginning of something greater than mission

3. **Ibid.**, p. 272.

walls. The twenty-one missions that grew and prospered along El Camino Real eventually crumbled. But their message never died.

If at first, in San Diego, the bells rang out in an empty world, their song reached hearts and souls yet to come. Primitive men came, heard and believed. Freed from the slavery of ignorance, hunger, filth and savagery, they learned a better way of life. In the mission, the Indian found protection, food, clothing, understanding and he found the freedom to become a man.

On August 28, 1784, the Apostle of California and one of America's great men slipped from this world into the infinite freedom of his God, but his brilliant example of hope, courage and faith established on the western shores of our continent a civilization that would blend into the American scene. As the colonists of the east were fighting for the Christian principles of independence, Serra was securing in California the ideal of man's dignity as a child of God and his right as an individual to pursue his talents. His memory lives on as do his fortitude and his sanctity.

ALTA CALIFORNIA MISSIONS
FOUNDED BY FATHER JUNIPERO SERRA

July 16, 1769	San Diego
June 3, 1770	San Carlos de Borromeo at Monterey
July 14, 1771	San Antonio de Padua
August 24, 1771	San Carlos de Borromeo moved to Carmel
September 8, 1771	San Gabriel
September 1, 1772	San Luis Obispo
October 29, 1775 November 1, 1776	San Juan Capistrano reestablished
October 9, 1776	San Francisco de Asis, Mission Dolores
January 12, 1777	Santa Clara
March 31, 1782	San Buenaventura

BIBLIOGRAPHY

Baer, Kurt, & Rudinger, Hugo P.
Architecture of the California Missions
University of California Press, Berkeley, Calif., 1958.
Berger, John A.
The Franciscan Missions of California
Doubleday & Co., Inc., Garden City, N.Y., 1948.
Bauer, Helen
California Mission Days
Doubleday & Co., Inc., Garden City, N.Y., 1951
California Rancho Days
Doubleday & Co., Inc., Garden City, N.Y., 1953.
Bolton, Herbert Eugene
Anza's California Expedition, 5 vols.
University of California Press, Berkeley, Calif., 1930.
Fray Juan Crespi, Missionary Explorer on the Pacific Coast
University of California Press, Berkeley, Calif., 1927.
Coronado — Knight of Pueblos and Plains
Whittlesey House, New York, N.Y., 1949.
Fray Francisco Palou, Vols. I, II, III, IV
Historical Memoirs of New California, Translated, Edited by H.
E. Bolton, From Manuscripts in Archives, Mexico, University of
California Press, Berkeley, Calif., 1926.
Missions as a Frontier in the Spanish American Colonies
Western College Press, El Paso, Texas, 1960.
Rim of Christendom
The Macmillan Co., New York, N.Y., 1936.
Padre of Horseback
The Sonora Press, San Francisco, Calif., 1932.
Spanish Explorations of the Southwest
C. Scribner's Sons, New York, N.Y., 1916.
Brandt, J. A.
Toward the New Spain
University of Chicago Press, Chicago, Ill., 1933.
Bro, Bernard, O.P.
The Spirituality of the Sacraments
Sheed & Ward, New York, N.Y., 1968.
Buell, R.
California Stepping Stones
Stanford University Press, Palo Alto, Calif., 1948.
Cannon, Ray and Sunset Editors
Sea of Cortez
Lane Magazine and Book Co., Menlo Park, Calif., 1966.

Chapman, Charles Edward
  Founding of Spanish California
  Macmillan Co., New York, N.Y., 1921.
  History of Spain
  Macmillan Co., New York, N.Y., 1918.
  Colonial Hispanic America
  Macmillan Co., New York, N.Y., 1933.
Chevignard, B. M., O.P.
  Reconciled With God
  Sheed & Ward, New York, N.Y., 1967.
Cicognani, Amleto Giovanni
  Sanctity in America
  St. Anthony Guild, Paterson, N.J., 1939.
Corle, Edwin
  The Gila, River of the Southwest
  Rinehart, New York, N.Y. (Holt, Rinehart & Winston, University
  of Nebraska Press, Lincoln, Neb.), 1951.
Collins, W.
  Cathedral Cities of Spain
  Dodd & Mead, Co., New York, N.Y., 1909.
Cullen, Rev. Th. F.
  Spirit of Serra
  Spiritual Books Associated, New York, N.Y., 1935.
Dawson, H. Christopher
  The Formation of Christendom
  Sheed & Ward, New York, N.Y., 1964.
Diez, Del Corral
  Majorca
  Norton, New York, N.Y., 1963.
Duffus, R. L.
  The Santa Fe Trail
  Tudor Publishing Co., New York, N.Y., 1963.
Englehardt, Zephrin, O.F.M.
  The Franciscans in California
  Holy Childhood Indian School, Harbor Springs, Mich., 1897.
  The Missions and Missionaries of California
  James H. Barry Co., San Francisco, Calif., 1916.
  Santa Barbara Mission
  James H. Barry Co., San Francisco, Calif., 1923.
  San Carlos de Borremeo
  The Schauer Printing Studio, Inc., Santa Barbara, Calif., 1934.
Farrell, Walter, O.P.
  A Companion to the Summa, 4 vols.
  Sheed & Ward, New York, N.Y., 1945-1951.

Fitch, A. H.
Junipero Serra
McClurg & Co., Chicago, Ill., 1914.
Garces, Francisco
On the Trail of a Spanish Pioneer, Diary of an Itinerary Priest
F. P. Harper, New York, N.Y., 1930, Revised: J. Howell Books,
San Francisco, Calif., 1965.
Gardner, Earle Stanley
The Hidden Heart of Baja
Wm. Morrow Co., New York, N.Y., 1968.
Hovering Over Baja
Wm. Morrow Co., New York, N.Y., 1962.
Geiger, Maynard J., O.F.M.; Ph.D.
The Life and Times of Junipero Serra, 2 vols.
Academy of American Franciscan History, The Wm. Byrd Press,
Inc., Richmond, Va., 1959.
Palou's Life of Fray Junipero Serra
Trans. with Notes, Academy of American Franciscan History, The
William Byrd Press Inc., Richmond, Va., 1955.
Gemelli, Agostino
The Franciscan Message to the World
Burns, London, 1934.
Hielscher, Kurt
Picturesque Spain
Brentano's, New York, N.Y., 1924.
Horgan, Paul
Conquistadors
Farrar, Strauss & Co., New York, N.Y., 1963.
The Great River — The Rio Grande
The Indians and Spain
Mexico and the United States
Funk & Wagnels, Div. Readers' Digest Books, Inc., Pleasantville,
N.Y., 1954-1968.
Hoffman, L. B.
California Beginnings
Harr Wagner, San Francisco, Calif., 1933.
Hurlimann, Martin
Spain
Viking Press, New York, N.Y., 1964.
James, George Wharton, Translation
Palou's Life of Junipero Serra
George Wharton James, Pasadena, Calif., 1913.
Kroeber, Alfred Louis
Handbook of the Indians of California

California Book Co., Ltd., Berkeley, Calif., 1953.
Krutch, Joseph Wood
Baja California and The Geography of Hope
Sierra Club Press, San Francisco, Calif., 1967.
Lummis, Charles Fletcher
Spanish Pioneer & California Missions
A. C. McClurg & Co., Chicago, Ill., 1929.
Madariaga, Salvador de
Spain, A Modern History
Frederick A. Praeger, Publishers, New York, N.Y., 1958.
Mais, S. P. B. and Gillian Mais
Majorcan Holiday
Books for Libraries Press, Freeport, N.Y., 1968.
Maass
The Dream of Phillip II
Bobbs-Merrill Co., Indianapolis, N.Y., 1945.
Maynard, Theodore
The Long Road
Appleton-Century-Crofts, Inc., New York, N.Y., 1954.
O'Brien, Eric
Apostle of California — Padre Serra
The Tidings Press, Los Angeles, Calif., 1944.
Prescott, W. H.
History of the Reign of Phillip II
J. B. Lippencott Co., Philadelphia, Pa., 1887.
History of the Conquest of Mexico
D. McKay, Philadelphia, Pa., 1893.
Repplier, Agnes
Junipero Serra, Pioneer Colonist of California
Doubleday & Doran Co., Inc., Garden City, N.Y., 1933.
Reynolds, James
Fabulous Spain
G. P. Putnam's Sons, New York, N.Y., 1953.
Richman, Irving B.
California Under Spain and Mexico
Houghton-Mifflin Co., Boston & New York, N.Y., 1911.
Rops, Daniel Henri
Cathedral and Crusade
E. P. Dutton & Co., Inc., New York, 1957.
Salter, Cedric
Introducing Spain
Sloane Co., New York, N.Y., 1953.
Shippen, Katherine B.
New Found World

The Viking Press, New York, N.Y., 1945, revised 1964.
Smith, Rhea Marsh
Spain
Univ. of Michigan Press, Ann Arbor, Mich., 1965.
Solhenitzn, Aleksander I
The First Circle, trans. from Russian, T. P. Whitney
Harper & Row, New York, N.Y., 1968.
Tibesar, Antonine, O.F.M., Ph.D.
Writings of Junipero Serra, 3 vols.
Academy of American Franciscan History, Washington, D.C., J. H.
Furst Co., Baltimore, Md., 1956.
Walsh, Marie T.
The Mission Bells of California
Harr Wagner Publishing Co., San Francisco, Calif., 1934.
Waxman, Percy
What Price Majorca
Farrar & Rinehart Inc., New York, N.Y., 1933.
The California Missions
Paul C. Johnson, Editor, Lane Magazine & Book Co., Menlo Park,
Calif., 1968.

INDEX

agriculture:
  Majorcan: 18
Alaska: 172
Alta California: 78, 81
Angel Island: 171
Angelus: 1
Anza, Col. Don Juan
  Bautista de: 154, 160-163, 172
  colonists: 176-177, 182
Apaches: 65, 162, 163
aqueducts: 83
Arabian horses: 65
Arabs: death of Lull: 12
  conquest: 20
Arizona: 161
Ayala, Capt. Juan Bautista de: 170

Baja California: 72, 81-84, 94,
  133, 163, 178, 191
  Indian boy: 126
baptism, first: 126
Barracar Ave.
  Serra home: 15-17
Bautista, Juan
  Indian boy: 150-154, 158-159
Beadle: 9
bear hunt: 143
bells, Palma: 1
  Loreto: 82
  Monterey: 115
  San Antonio: 129
  San Juan Capistrano: 179
  Carmel: 207

Bon Any, shrine: 37, 38
Bucareli, Viceroy: 148, 154, 157,
  163, 166, 169, 177
  northern exped.: 172
  death: 189
Bueno: 113, 114
Brazil, slaves: 52

Cabrillo: 78, 97
Cadiz: 40, 41
California
  discovery: 78
  Serra's vision: 124
Cambon, Father: 128, 134, 146
Campa, Father: 92, 94
Canada, fur traders: 65
Carlos, King: 69, 170
Carmel river: 106, 114
Carmelite Fathers: 115
Carquinez Straight: 142
Carthegenian occupation: 20
Catalan: 20
Catalonia: 20, 22
Cathedral, Palma: 9, 26
Cavaller, Father: 128, 144
Celts: 20
Cermeno, Capt.: 171
Chaquet, Capt. Diego de: 185
Charles, King: 54, 77
Chronicles, Seraphic Order: 27
colonization: 176, 177
  Neve: 200
Comanches: 65, 66, 161, 162

217